Python for Information Professionals

How to Design Applications to Capitalize on the Data Explosion

Brady D. Lund
Daniel Agbaji
Kossi Dodzi Bissadu
Haihua Chen

ROWMAN & LITTLEFIELD
Lanham • Boulder • New York • London

Acquisitions Editor: Charles Harmon
Acquisitions Assistant: Lauren Moynihan
Sales and Marketing Inquiries: textbooks@rowman.com

Credits and acknowledgments for material borrowed from other sources, and reproduced with permission, appear on the appropriate pages within the text.

Published by Rowman & Littlefield
An imprint of The Rowman & Littlefield Publishing Group, Inc.
4501 Forbes Boulevard, Suite 200, Lanham, Maryland 20706
www.rowman.com

86-90 Paul Street, London EC2A 4NE

Copyright © 2024 by The Rowman & Littlefield Publishing Group, Inc.

All rights reserved. No part of this book may be reproduced in any form or by any electronic or mechanical means, including information storage and retrieval systems, without written permission from the publisher, except by a reviewer who may quote passages in a review.

British Library Cataloguing in Publication Information Available

Library of Congress Cataloging-in-Publication Data

Names: Lund, Brady, 1994- author. | Agbaji, Daniel, author. | Bissadu, Kossi Dodzi, author. | Chen, Haihua, author.
Title: Python for information professionals : how to design practical applications to capitalize on the data explosion / Brady Lund, Daniel Agbaji, Kossi Dodzi Bissadu, Haihua Chen.
Description: Lanham : Rowman & Littlefield Publishers, [2024] | Includes bibliographical references and index.
Identifiers: LCCN 2023031250 (print) | LCCN 2023031251 (ebook) | ISBN 9781538178249 (cloth) | ISBN 9781538178256 (paperback) | ISBN 9781538178263 (ebook)
Subjects: LCSH: Python (Computer program language) | Libraries—Data processing.
Classification: LCC Z678.93.P98 L86 2024 (print) | LCC Z678.93.P98 (ebook) | DDC 025.00285—dc23/eng20231013
LC record available at https://lccn.loc.gov/2023031250
LC ebook record available at https://lccn.loc.gov/2023031251

Contents

Preface v

Part I: Python: The Basics

Chapter 1: The Python Workspace 3

Chapter 2: Object-Oriented Programming 13

Chapter 3: Data Types, Structures, Sets, and Algorithms 27

Chapter 4: Functions: Code That Puts Our Data to Work 37

Chapter 5: Importing, Creating, and Maintaining Data Files 47

Chapter 6: Testing and Troubleshooting 57

Part II: Further Applications of Python in Information Organizations

Chapter 7: Library Management and Usage Data 69

Chapter 8: Library Research Data Management 81

Chapter 9: Text Analysis 91

Chapter 10: Library and Information Science Research 101

Chapter 11: Artificial Intelligence Applications 111

Part III: Practical and Ethical Considerations for Using Python

Chapter 12: Data Explosion, Big Data, and Data Literacy 121

Chapter 13: Data Ethics 129

Chapter 14: Knowledge and Data Economy 137

Chapter 15: Further Resources for Advancing Your Python Mastery 147

Glossary 155

Index 157

About the Authors 161

Preface

Welcome, reader. We are glad you have chosen this resource to support you as you learn about one of the most valuable skill sets for the modern data or information professional, the Python programming language. In this book, we endeavor to introduce you to the basics of Python, in addition to some advanced concepts, as well as contextualize this learning by presenting relevant examples for the library and information sciences. We have intentionally designed this book so that it begins with simpler concepts and then builds in complexity, such that you will be able to follow along regardless of where you are in your Python learning. This book can be used as a learning resource for beginners, or a ready reference for those looking for a few pointers to improve their coding abilities.

In this introduction to the book, we aim to explore the fundamental aspects of Python, its immense popularity, and the reasons why it is crucial for you to learn and master it. By doing so, we will provide you with a solid foundation for the rest of the book, which will enable you to take your skills to the next level and achieve your goals. It is vital to learn Python, as it is rapidly becoming the de facto language for many industries and applications during the data revolution, with Python programmers being in high demand among large companies as well as information organizations like public and academic libraries. By mastering Python, you will not only acquire a valuable skill set that will benefit you in your current or future career but also gain the ability to create useful tools and applications that can improve your daily life.

WHY PYTHON?

Some readers may ask, "Why Python specifically? What makes you select this language over its many rivals?" There are several ways to answer this question. One way is to simply point to the popularity of the language. Figure 0.1 shows Google Trends (2023) data for the popularity of searches relating to three common coding languages: Java, C, and Python. For most of the last two decades, Java was king. However, since mid-2019, Python has taken the dominant role among the three languages, even though it was hardly an afterthought to both Java and C for over a decade (2004–2014). Over the past five years, Python has

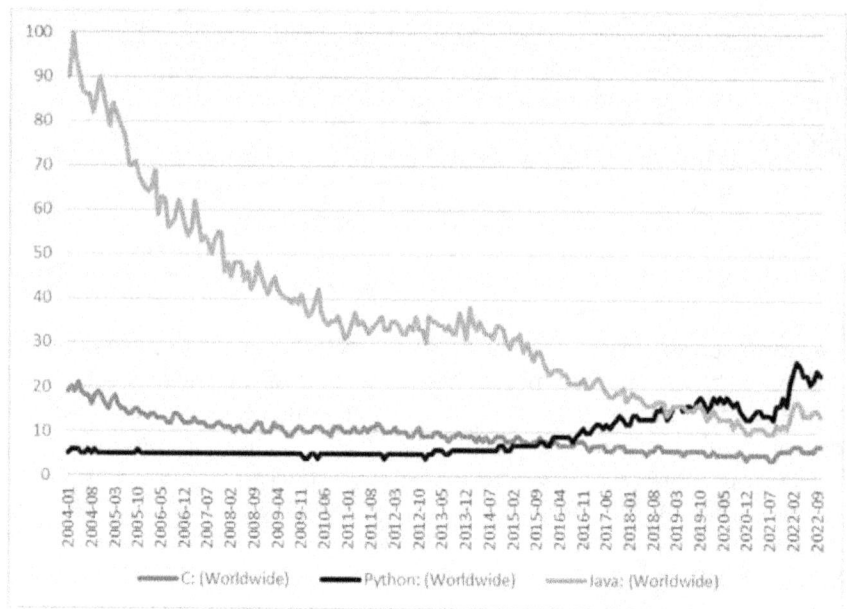

Figure 0.1. Google Trends for Searches Relating to C, Java, and Python
Source: The authors

been the most popular search among the three languages in all but a handful of countries (Brazil, India, Spain, Mexico, Saudi Arabia, and Nigeria), and in the year 2022, it was the single most popular coding language in all but two countries worldwide (Mexico and Nigeria).

A second way to explain the language's popularity is its versatility and extensive library of modules, frameworks, and tools that make it the go-to language for developers worldwide. Python's vast ecosystem supports a variety of applications, ranging from web development to scientific computing, data analysis, and machine learning. It has several libraries dedicated to specific domains, such as NumPy, Pandas, and Matplotlib, which facilitate data analysis and visualization, and TensorFlow, Keras, and PyTorch, which support machine-learning applications.

Additionally, Python is a free and open-source language, which means that anyone can use it without licensing costs, and its source code is available to everyone to modify, improve, and redistribute. This feature of Python has spawned the growth of a lively community of developers committed to the continuous improvement of the Python language, with regular updates and bug fixes. The language can work across a variety of operating systems—Windows, Linux, and macOS—and it integrates easily with other programming languages like C and C++.

WHAT IS PYTHON?

Python is a high-level, general-purpose programming language, meaning that it can be used for a variety of purposes and tasks, unlike a language like HTML, which is a markup language used specifically for the purpose of structuring content on the web. Python can be used for a wide range of applications, including web development, scientific computing, machine learning, and data analysis, among others. Python's syntax is designed to be readable and easy to use, making it an ideal language for beginners and experts alike.

Python was created by Guido van Rossum in the late 1980s, with the first version of Python being released in 1991 (Millman & Aivazis, 2011). The language is named after the British comedy group Monty Python, and its creator's fondness for the group's humor is evident in the language's documentation and examples. It is a versatile language that supports multiple programming paradigms, including procedural, functional, and object-oriented programming. Procedural programming involves executing code step-by-step, using procedures or functions to complete a task. Functional programming emphasizes composing functions to perform computations, with an emphasis on immutability. Object-oriented programming involves organizing code into objects that contain both data and methods for utilizing the data. Python's support for multiple programming paradigms makes it a flexible language that can be adapted to suit a wide range of needs and applications. Object-oriented programming will be a major focus of this book and is discussed in greater detail in chapter 3.

WHAT CAN PYTHON DO?

Python is an incredibly versatile language that finds applications in various domains. It is extensively used in web development, thanks to frameworks like Django and Flask, which simplify the creation of dynamic websites and web applications. Python's rich ecosystem of libraries, such as NumPy, Pandas, and Matplotlib, enables efficient data manipulation, analysis, and visualization, making it a popular choice for data science and analytics. With libraries like TensorFlow, Keras, and scikit-learn, Python facilitates machine learning and artificial-intelligence tasks, providing tools for model building and training. Python's simplicity and ease of use make it suitable for scripting, automation, and system administration, while libraries like SciPy and SymPy support scientific computing and simulation. Python's Pygame library enables game development, and it can also be used for IoT applications, desktop application development, and building cross-platform graphical user interfaces.

PYTHON FOR LIBRARIANS AND INFORMATION PROFESSIONALS

Python has gained significant popularity among librarians and information professionals due to its versatility and usefulness in various library practices.

The following are several successful examples of Python applications in this field. Each of these topics will be discussed in greater detail within the chapters that follow.

1. Data Manipulation and Analysis: Librarians can harness the power of Python's robust data manipulation and analysis libraries, such as Pandas and NumPy, to organize and scrutinize vast datasets (Ranjani et al., 2019). This empowers them to uncover invaluable insights into library usage, optimize collection-management strategies, and gain a deeper understanding of user behavior.
2. Web Scraping and Data Extraction: Equipped with Python's versatile libraries, like BeautifulSoup and Scrapy, librarians can effortlessly extract valuable data from websites and online catalogs (Thomas & Mathur, 2019). This functionality proves invaluable in gathering comprehensive information about books, articles, and various resources, ensuring an enriched and up-to-date collection.
3. Text Mining and Natural Language Processing: Python's NLTK (Natural Language Toolkit) and spaCy libraries open avenues for librarians to delve into text mining and natural-language processing. Leveraging these tools, librarians can extract meaningful information from textual resources, perform sentiment analysis, and streamline processes like cataloging with automated capabilities.
4. Automation of Routine Tasks: With Python's scripting capabilities at their disposal, librarians can automate repetitive tasks that plague their workflows. This includes streamlining batch processing of files, efficient file renaming, and meticulous data cleaning, thereby saving valuable time and boosting overall operational efficiency (Graser & Burel, 2019).
5. Digital Preservation: Python serves as a reliable companion in digital preservation endeavors. Librarians can utilize its capabilities for critical tasks such as file-format conversions, metadata extraction, and efficient digital-asset management. Libraries like PyMARC and PyPDF2 prove instrumental in seamlessly handling the diverse file formats commonly encountered in library environments.
6. User Interaction and Services: Python empowers librarians to create interactive and user-centric experiences. By leveraging its capabilities, they can develop chatbots, recommendation systems, and interactive interfaces tailored to the needs of library users. These tools enhance user engagement, provide personalized services, and create an enriched environment for exploration and discovery (Lyons, 2019).
7. Integration with Library Systems: Python seamlessly integrates with various library-management systems and discovery tools, granting librarians the freedom to develop custom functionalities and automate workflows (Lou,

2023). This integration enhances efficiency, optimizes processes, and ultimately elevates the overall user experience within the library ecosystem.

These are but a handful of the many possible uses of Python in libraries that will be explored throughout this book!

HOW DOES THIS BOOK DIFFER FROM OTHER PYTHON TEXTS?

While there is no shortage of books available for learning Python, this book offers a unique approach and presents the material in a way that is accessible and easy to understand. Unlike most other Python resources, this book takes a targeted approach to Python programming, looking at its applications within a specific discipline—library and information science—and its affiliated professions. It also differs from other books on the market in practical and accessible style. We have made the effort to avoid overuse of jargon and instead describe things in a straightforward manner that will be approachable for all readers. For readers who have struggled with other books and online courses, we hope this will be the resource that finally helps you to master this tremendous language.

OUTLINE OF THIS BOOK

This book is a comprehensive guide to learning Python programming language from the basics to advanced concepts. The book is divided into three parts, with each part focusing on a specific aspect of Python's application. The first part of the book is an introduction to the Python programming language, discussing its history, features, and importance in the information profession. This section is designed for beginners to Python and focuses on the fundamentals of the language. The first chapter will orient you to the Python workspace and various options in terms of platforms for practicing and using Python. Next, we will discuss object-oriented programming and how it is used with Python. This will be followed by a chapter focusing on data types, structures, sets, and algorithms, a key component of Python for data-science applications. Following this introduction, we will round out part 1 of the book by discussing functions, as well as how to import, create, and maintain your data files, and how to test and troubleshoot your code.

The second part of the book explores various applications of Python in information organizations. Each chapter focuses on a different area of library and information science and how Python can be utilized in practical ways to improve processes and outcomes. This section is intended for those who want to apply Python in their work or research in library and information science. One chapter is included for each of the following topics/challenges that might be faced within library and information organizations: library management and usage data, library research data, text analysis, library and information-science research, and artificial-intelligence applications.

The third and final part of the book is focused on practical considerations for using Python with organizational and research data. The chapters in this section aim to help readers understand the ethical implications of working with data, as well as the broader economic impact of quality data. The first of these chapters focuses on the issues of the data explosion, the growth of big data, and the need for data literacy in the modern world. Next, we explore ethical issues related to data and data science. The final chapter in this section explores the economic value of data and opportunities for data scientists and data librarians.

The book concludes with a summary of the topics covered and provides additional resources for further learning. The chapters are designed to be approachable and easy to follow, with each chapter building on the concepts presented in previous chapters. By the end of the book, readers will have a strong foundation in the Python programming language and will be equipped with the knowledge and skills needed to apply it in real-world scenarios.

Learning Python is an invaluable skill in today's data-driven world, and this book is an excellent resource for anyone looking to master it. We look forward to taking you on a journey from the basics of Python programming all the way to advanced concepts and enhancing this content through real-world examples and datasets from the world of library and information science. By the end of the book, you will have the skills and confidence you need to start writing your own Python programs and be well on your way to becoming a proficient Python programmer! So, pull up to your computer, and let us begin!

REFERENCES

Google Trends. (2023, May 21). R, C++, Python. Retrieved from https://trends.google.com/trends/.

Graser, M., & Burel, M. (2019). Metadata Automation: The Current Landscape and Future Developments. *Bulletin: Vol. 45*(2), 4.

Lou, D. (2023). Using Python scripts to compare records from vendors with those from ILS. *Code4Lib, 55.* https://journal.code4lib.org/articles/17022.

Lyons, K. R. (2019). AxoPy: A Python library for implementing human-computer interface experiments. *Journal of Open Source Software, 4*(34), 1191.

Millman, K., & Aivazis, M. (2011). Python for scientists and engineers. *Computing in Science and Engineering, 13*(2), 9–12.

Ranjani, J., Sheela, A., & Meena, K. P. (2019, April). Combination of NumPy, SciPy and Matplotlib/Pylab—a good alternative methodology to MATLAB—A comparative analysis. In *2019 1st International Conference on Innovations in Information and Communication Technology (ICIICT)* (pp. 1–5). IEEE.

Thomas, D. M., & Mathur, S. (2019, June). Data analysis by web scraping using Python. In *2019 3rd International Conference on Electronics, Communication and Aerospace Technology (ICECA)* (pp. 450–54). IEEE.

Part I

Python

The Basics

1

The Python Workspace

In this chapter, our focus will be on preparing our computer or workstation for coding in the Python programming language. We will explore the various workspaces available for developing Python libraries. As a Python developer, it is essential to have the right tools for success. We will discuss both free and open-source options, as well as proprietary tools that may require financial commitments. By the end of this chapter, you will have a comprehensive understanding of Python development workspaces and how to use them effectively. We will also cover industry best practices for using these tools in a professional setting, equipping you with the necessary knowledge and skills to excel as a Python developer.

Before we delve into the different workspaces for Python development, let us first discuss a bit about how the Python programming language functions. (This is just a brief introduction, as we will discuss these topics in greater detail in future chapters.) We will explore the activities involved, from writing lines of code to executing them and obtaining the desired results. Having a basic understanding of how Python works can be helpful in troubleshooting any issues you may encounter during code writing and execution.

HOW PYTHON WORKS

As discussed in the introduction of this book, it is important to understand that Python is an Object-Oriented Programming (OOP) language. An OOP is a computer-programming approach that organizes software design or development around objects or data, rather than functions and logic (Rentsch, 1982). The basic structure of an OOP includes classes, objects, methods, and attributes. Classes are user-defined data types that act like template definition of methods and attributes of an individual object. An object is an instance of a class that consists of methods and properties created with specifically defined data. A

Table 1.1. Structural Elements of an OOP with an Example

Structural Elements	Example
Class	A dog
Object	The name of the dog
Properties	The color of the dog
Method	Bark

method is a function that is defined within a class that describes the behavior of an object. An attribute represents the state of an object. Table 1.1 gives you a simple example of the structural elements of an OOP.

Python codes are structured in such a way that they follow a boilerplate that describes instances of the Python class you create as object. Think of an object in Python as a copy of the boilerplate code you have created. Just like any other object in our physical environment, Python objects can be described, be called by name, or even use its functions to carry out a task in the program you write (Lutz, 2013). This concept and many others will be fully dealt with in subsequent chapters. For now, it is important to understand that the concept of Python programming language being called an OOP language is because it treats the code you create as an object. This could be the entire class of codes or even a block of codes. This means that the code you develop in Python can be reused like every other object, modified, and even encapsulated. And like most OOP languages out there, it follows a similar pattern of features and functionality. Understanding how Python works is key to knowing why Python code functions the way it does and why the workspace should be equipped with the right resources to build Python codes. Also, this understanding will create a better appreciation for using Python as a programming language in building functional applications for a library or any information service-providing organization where you work.

Therefore, let us break the Python programming layers of operations (how the language works) down to a summary of steps that provides a mental picture of how Python as an OOP language works. The following diagram describes the various steps or layers involved in Python programming—from the moment a single line of code is written to the time when it is executed by the computer.

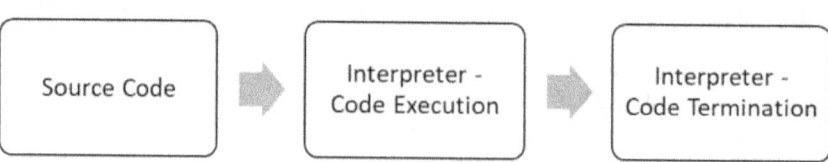

Figure 1.1. Summary of How Python Programming Works
Source: The authors

From the diagram above, you will notice that the source code you write in Python is the first layer in the functionality of Python codes. Hence, writing clean codes means the Python programming language can understand what you have written and will execute it. To run a code means to send your source code to Python for execution. But that's not the end to the steps in the functionality of Python as a programming language. The Python interpreter is the next in the steps. It is preinstalled with your Python programming language. Hence, you do not need a separate installation for the interpreter. As the name implies, it is responsible for interpreting the code from the human-related language, in this case Python programming language to the machine language, also known as low-level language. The machine language is the language the computer understands.

These interpretation features provided by the Python interpreter help execute the code you have written and run. However, there are quite a few things the interpreter does "under the hood" to execute your code successfully. Part of the behind-the-scenes work the interpreter does is to break the codes you have written into tokens, or smaller units, then to parse those tokens into a structural pattern that it uses to identify all the various features of the codes you have written. Once the interpreter has gotten a better understanding of the code you have written, then it passes what it has gotten into an Abstract Syntax Tree (AST). The AST holds byte codes. The byte code, also known as the 0s and 1s language the computer understands, is then generated from the AST so the computer can understand the instruction you have written in the Python code. To achieve this objective, once the code is done executing, the result is then provided. The interpreter ends the execution of the code once the process is complete.

THE PYTHON WORKSPACE

The Python workspace plays a critical role in the development of Python programs. It refers to the digital environment where Python code is designed, developed, and executed, and it consists of several essential elements. To write Python code, you can use any text-formatting application that doesn't add unnecessary metadata to the code. In this chapter, we will refer to such text-formatting applications as "plain" text-formatting applications. However, it's important to note that most plain text-formatting applications don't provide the functionality to run the code within the same environment.

For the Windows Operating System, examples of plain text-formatting applications that can be used to write Python code are Notepad and Notepad Plus (Notepad++). On the MacOS, a plain text-formatting application called TextEdit can be used to develop Python code and code in other programming languages. There are also other plain text-formatting applications or software that can be installed on your operating system to develop Python code.

Now, let's say you used Notepad, Notepad Plus, or TextEdit to write some lines of code. Although you can view the code within the same environment, you cannot run or compile it for the computer to understand. This is where a compiler/interpreter comes in. A compiler or interpreter is essential for running your Python code. It translates high-level programming source code into machine code that the computer can comprehend. While a compiler generates assembly-like program code, an interpreter executes code line by line, producing results from the program. In other words, a compiler produces intermediate machine codes, while an interpreter reads and executes individual lines of code.

PYTHON WORKSPACE USING PLAIN TEXT-FORMATTING APPLICATION

To write and execute Python codes using a plain text-formatting environment would require the use of the Python Command Line Interface (CLI). The Python CLI can be accessed via the terminal application (in MacOS) or via the Command Prompt Interface (in Windows OS). The Python CLI comes preinstalled with most operating systems, and it comes as part of the Python package when you install Python. The following steps can be followed to execute Python codes when written in a plain text-formatting environment:

1. After writing your code in the plain text-formatting environment, ensure that it is syntax and logic error-free; then save the file with a ".py" extension in a folder you can easily access.
2. Now, open the Command Line Prompt, also known as the "CMD" in Windows OS, and Terminal in MacOS. To open the Command Line Prompt in Windows OS, select the Windows start button and type the key word "CMD." This will bring up the CMD application in the search bar. You can then click on it to open the application. In MacOS, you can access the terminal by pulling up the "Spotlight" interface and then type in the keyword "Terminal." On MacOS PCs, the spotlight interface can be pulled up by simply typing the command and space-bar key simultaneously on your keyboard. In the search bar, type in the key word "Terminal."
3. Once you have the Command Line Interface opened on your preferred PC, then navigate to the location of the Python code file you saved in step one, by typing the CD (Change Directory) command. For instance, if you saved the file in the documents folder, then typing the command "CD Document" will point the Command Line Interface to the document folder where the file is located.
4. Now that you are within the directory where the Python code file is saved, you can execute the code by calling the Python command, "Python" followed by the name of the file that contains the code. Say the name of the file is saved as "books.py"; then the Python execution command will look like this: "Python books.py."

5. After the code is done executing, the Python interpreter will return the result of the code in the next line of the Command Line Interface.

PYTHON WORKSPACE USING INTEGRATED DEVELOPMENT ENVIRONMENT

Unlike using a plain text-formatting application as a workspace for developing Python codes, most Python workspaces come as a single combined piece of environment. This is usually referred to as Integrated Development Environment. An Integrated Development Environment (IDE) is an essential part of the Python workspace. An IDE provides a comprehensive and intelligent integrated environment for coding, testing, and debugging Python code. It offers features such as code highlighting, autocompletion, error reporting, and debugging tools, among others. Some popular Python IDEs include PyCharm, Spyder, and Jupyter Notebook.

The Standard Development Kit (SDK) is also an important part of the Python workspace. The SDK provides a set of tools and libraries that enable the development and deployment of Python applications. The SDK typically includes a compiler, a debugger, libraries, and other tools that are necessary for developing and testing Python code.

Plugins, or extensions, are additional components that can be added to the Python workspace to enhance its functionality. For example, plugins can be used to add support for specific programming languages, integrate with other development tools, or provide additional debugging and testing capabilities.

Finally, the operating system is also an important component of the Python workspace. Python is supported on various operating systems, including Windows, MacOS, and Linux. The operating system provides the underlying infrastructure that supports the execution of Python code and the other components of the Python workspace.

When it comes to hardware, developers can choose to use a physical computer or a virtual machine, or cloud computing. Python is preinstalled on most operating systems and can be run using the Command Line Interface on various devices like PCs, Macs, and Chromebooks. However, to ensure smooth operation, the hardware should meet the minimum specifications, including RAM memory and CPU speed. These requirements can vary depending on the complexity of the programs being developed and the amount of data being processed.

Table 1.2 provides a general overview of the minimum hardware specifications required to develop Python programs. However, it is not an exhaustive list, and developers can choose to use more memory and CPU power if needed.

When it comes to software, it is important to confirm whether the Python programming language, also known as the Python CLI, is installed on your computer. The next section will provide step-by-step instructions on how to confirm and install Python on both MacOS and Windows.

Table 1.2. Hardware Specifications Requirements for Developing with Python (Python System Requirements—TAE, 2022)

Operating System and Version	CPU Architecture	RAM and Free Disk Space
Windows PC, Version 7 or higher MacOS X 10.11 or higher Linux: RHEL 6/7, 64-bit	At least a Dual Core Intel Core i5 or higher	At least 4G RAM At least 5G disk space

INSTALLATION OF PYTHON PROGRAMMING LANGUAGE ON A LOCAL COMPUTER

Assuming you want to set up a Python workspace on both a Windows PC and a MacOS computer, and both computers meet the minimum requirements specified in Table 1.2, the next step is to confirm whether the Python programming language is preinstalled on your computer. The version of Python running on your computer is important, as some versions may not be compatible with the version of your operating system (Python Releases for Windows, 2023; Python Releases for MacOS, 2023).

To check whether Python is installed on a Windows PC, follow these steps:

1. Navigate to the Windows button and click on it to open the Windows dialog display.
2. Type "Command Prompt" or "CMD" in the search bar.
3. Hit the enter key on the keyboard to open the Windows Command Prompt (CMD) Interface.
4. Type "Python—version" in the CMD Interface to check if Python is installed and find its version number.

To check whether Python is installed on a MacOS computer, follow these steps:

1. Navigate to the Mac Launchpad by clicking on the Launchpad icon on the taskbar or by using the key combination "Space + Command" and typing "Launchpad."
2. On the search bar, type "terminal" to open the Mac Terminal, which serves the same purpose as the Windows CMD/Command Prompt Interface.
3. Type "Python—version" in the Terminal to find the version of Python currently running on your computer.

If Python is not installed on your computer, the next step is to install it. Before installing, it is important to check whether the version of Python you want to run on your computer is compatible with your operating system (Python Releases for Windows, 2023; Python Releases for MacOS, 2023). For example, in this case, we will download and install version 3 of Python on Windows and MacOS computers.

To install Python on a Windows PC:

1. Open a browser and search for "Download Python."
2. Find the official Python download page from the search results and locate the appropriate version for your operating system.
3. Download the Python installer to a folder on your computer.
4. Double-click on the downloaded Python installer file to start the installation process.
5. Follow the installation wizard to install Python version 3.11.2 on your computer.

For MacOS computers, a popular package manager is Homebrew, which can be used to manage packages installed on the computer. To install Homebrew and Python on a MacOS computer:

1. Copy the Homebrew installer Bash script from the official website.
2. Paste the script in the MacOS Terminal and hit the return key.
3. Confirm the installation by typing "brew" in the Terminal, which will display all related Homebrew commands.
4. Type "brew install Python3" in the Terminal to install the Python interpreter.
5. Type "Python3" to confirm the installation of Python3 on your computer.

Installing Python or a package manager is just the first step in preparing a workspace for Python programming. In the next section, you will learn how to set up an Integrated Development Environment (IDE) for Python programming on your local computer.

SETTING UP AN IDE FOR PYTHON PROGRAMMING ON YOUR LOCAL COMPUTER

Installing the Python interpreter/compiler on your computer is one of many steps to preparing a Python development workspace. Securing an IDE that you can use and that is compatible with the Python programming language is essential to building the right workspace. So, what is this cool term called *IDE*? An IDE, also known as the Integrated Development Environment, is a piece of software, mostly a desktop application like Microsoft Word, that provides the flexibility of installing plugins/extensions, code completion or IntelliSense, code formatting or linting, code debugging, and even code execution. Most IDEs are designed for developing several programming languages.

There are many IDEs out there that you can use to build Python codes. Some of them are free, while others require some payment for licensing. Some examples are PyCharm, IntelliJ IDE, Eclipse, NetBeans, Visual Studio Code, etc. The list goes on and on. However, a popular IDE for your local computer is the Visual Studio Code (VSC), provided by Microsoft. It is free, and it comes with a user-friendly interface. You need to first download the VSC IDE from the official website to your local computer before you can start making use of it. As of this date, the official page for downloading VSC has the URL https://code.visualstudio.com/Download. Once there, select the installation file appropriate for your operating system.

To prepare the VSC IDE for Python programming, you will need to install the appropriate extensions for Python programming. Most of the extensions we will list here are provided by Microsoft, the same company responsible for VSC IDE. Locate the extension/package icon, mostly found on the left side of the IDE, then search and install the following list of extensions:

1. Python: This extension provides IntelliSense, code linting, code debugging, and some other excellent features that the default Python installation does not provide.
2. Python Preview: This is a Python debugger extension tool. It provides a visual and interactive feeling of debugging Python codes.
3. Jupyter: If you like the popular Jupyter Notebook interface that provides a user-friendly and effortless way to write and run Python codes, then this extension will add up as one of your essential tools for programming in Python within the VSC IDE.
4. Tabnine: This is a code completion extension tool, with IntelliSense features for developing artificial intelligence-related codes.
5. Python Test Explorer for Visual Studio Code: This extension provides unit testing of your Python codes. With this extension, you can run a test to check whether your Python program is working correctly or not.

Outside the five examples of Python-related extensions for VSC IDE mentioned above, there are other popular extensions you may stumble upon. We suggest reading the reviews and verifying the author or company responsible for the extension before making a final decision about whether to install it or not. Also, you can use the number of times the extension has been downloaded by other developers to justify the decision to install or not to install.

Now that you have your local computer ready with an IDE installed for developing Python code, it is important to note that you can also build Python codes in the cloud. Knowing how to build Python codes in the cloud ensures that you can still build and run your code when you are not with the computer on which you installed the VSC IDE and other Python workspace-related tools. Some popular cloud-based workstations are Google Collab and Jupyter Notebook. These two cloud-based Python workspaces can help reduce the need to carry your computer with you. However, you must be connected to the Internet through another computer before you can gain access to the cloud workspace.

With your computer prepared for development, you can now move forward with developing your first lines of code!

REFERENCES

Lutz, M. (2013). *Learning Python: Powerful object-oriented programming.* O'Reilly Media.

Python Releases for MacOS. (2023). Retrieved March 6, 2023, from Python.org website: https://www.python.org/downloads/macos/.

Python Releases for Windows. (2023). Retrieved March 6, 2023, from Python.org website: https://www.python.org/downloads/windows/.

Python System Requirements—TAE. (2022). Retrieved March 6, 2023, from Tutorialandexample.com website: https://www.tutorialandexample.com/python-systemrequirements#:~:text=Python%20System%20Requirements%201%20Introduction%2020w%20know%2C,Prerequisites%3A%20...%207%20Installing%20Python%20on%20Lnux%20.

Rentsch, T. (1982). Object-oriented programming. ACM Sigplan Notices, 17(9), 51–57.

2

Object-Oriented Programming

The programming paradigm known as Object-Oriented Programming (OOP) is centered around the notion of "objects," which are instances of classes that contain both data and behavior (Cox, 1986). OOP emphasizes the development of modular and reusable code, making it easier to comprehend, maintain, and expand code. In OOP, programs are structured into classes, which serve as blueprints for objects. These classes contain attributes (variables that store data) and methods (functions that operate on the data). A key feature of OOP is encapsulation, which limits access to data and methods to only the class's public interface.

Python, as an OOP language, supports the creation of classes and objects, making it simpler for developers to generate code that is modular, reusable, and easy to comprehend (Lutz, 2010). OOP principles enable developers to break down complex problems into more manageable pieces, leading to more efficient and structured code. One significant benefit of OOP in Python is the ability to reuse code (Sanner, 1999). By defining classes and objects, code can be utilized in various parts of a program or even across multiple programs, reducing time and code duplication.

OOP enhances code organization by grouping related attributes and methods within a single class. This approach makes it easier to manage and modify code, resulting in better maintainability and scalability. In this chapter, we will look at the basics of OOP in the Python language, including concepts such as classes and objects, inheritance, and encapsulation. By comprehending these principles, developers can create more effective and efficient code and take advantage of the full potential of the Python language.

CLASSES AND OBJECTS

DEFINITION OF CLASS AND OBJECT

Classes and objects are fundamental concepts in Object-Oriented Programming (OOP) that facilitate the creation of modular and structured code. A class functions as a template or blueprint for producing objects. It specifies a set of attributes that describe the object's state, as well as methods that define the object's behavior. For instance, a Book class might contain attributes such as title, author, and ISBN, as well as methods like borrow and return.

Meanwhile, an object is an instance of a class that has particular values assigned to its attributes. Objects are generated from classes, and each object created from a class is unique and distinct from other objects of the same class. This implies that if you have a Book class, you can create two separate Book objects, each with its own attributes, such as title, author, and ISBN.

In Python, every element is an object, including built-in data types such as strings, integers, and lists (Oliphant, 2007). This means that even built-in data types have attributes and methods that can be used to manipulate them. By defining new classes, developers can create new data types that can be utilized to generate objects, making it feasible to build custom objects that represent real-world objects or concepts in their code.

By using classes and objects, developers can produce code that is reusable and well-organized, leading to easy maintenance and expansion. Additionally, OOP allows developers to encapsulate data and behavior within objects, which can make their code more secure and easier to understand.

CREATING AND USING CLASSES AND OBJECTS IN PYTHON

Creating a class in Python is straightforward. We start by using the class keyword, followed by the name of the class, and a colon. Then, we define the class's attributes and methods. Here is an example of a basic class in Python:

```
class Person:
    def __init__(self, name, age):
        self.name = name
        self.age = age
    def greet(self):
        print(f"Hello, my name is {self.name} and I'm
        {self.age} years old.")
```

In this example, we define a class called Person with two attributes, name and age, and a method called greet that prints out a message using the object's attributes. We use the special method __init__ to initialize the object's attributes when it is created.

To create an object of the Person class, we simply call the class like a function and pass in the required arguments:

```
person = Person("John", 30)
```

In this example, we create an object called Person with the name attribute set to "John" and the age attribute set to 30. We can then call the greet method on the object to print out the message:

```
person.greet()
```

This will print out the message:

"Hello, my name is John, and I'm 30 years old."

Title of Code Sample: Creating a class and object for a library spending account
Objective of Code Sample: The sample code below shows an example of how one can create a class and an object for a library spending account in Python.
Sample Code:
Initialize the class by using the keyword "class" followed by the name you would like to give the class; in this case, we named it "LibraryAccount".

```
class LibraryAccount:
    def __init__(self, budget):
       self.budget = budget
    def purchase(self, cost):
       if self.budget >= cost:
           self.budget -= cost
       else:
           print("Insufficient budget.")
```

Create an "account" object from the "LibraryAccount" class

```
account = LibraryAccount(1000)
account.purchase(500)
account.purchase(2000)
account.purchase(800)
print(account.budget)
```

In this example, we define a class called LibraryAccount with an attribute called budget and a method called purchase to modify the budget attribute. We create an object called account with an initial budget of 1000 and then make three purchases: one for 500, one for 2000 (which fails due to insufficient budget), and one for 800. The print statement at the end outputs the remaining budget, which should be 200.

INHERITANCE

DEFINITION OF INHERITANCE

Inheritance is a powerful feature in object-oriented programming that enables a class to inherit attributes and methods from another class. By doing so, inheritance promotes code reuse, reduces duplication, and helps with code organization. The class that is inherited from is commonly referred to as the parent class or superclass, while the class that inherits from it is known as the child class or subclass. The child class has access to all the attributes and methods of the parent class and can override or add its own attributes and methods. This allows the child class to inherit the behavior and attributes of the parent class, while also having the flexibility to modify it as required.

Using inheritance allows you to create new classes that are built on top of existing classes, rather than starting from scratch. This approach enables you to reuse the existing code and significantly reduces the amount of code that needs to be written. Consequently, your code becomes more efficient and easier to maintain. In Python, you can define a new class that inherits from an existing class using the class keyword. You can indicate the parent class by putting it in parentheses after the name of the child class. For example, if you have a parent class called Person with attributes name and age, you can create a child class called Student that inherits from the Person class and adds an additional attribute, student_id.

HOW TO IMPLEMENT INHERITANCE IN PYTHON

To implement inheritance in Python, we define a new class that inherits from an existing class using the following syntax:

```python
class ChildClass(ParentClass):
    def __init__(self, child_attribute, parent_attribute):
        super().__init__(parent_attribute)
        self.child_attribute = child_attribute
```

In the above example, we define a child class called ChildClass that inherits from a parent class called ParentClass. We use the super() function to call the parent class's __init__() method and initialize the parent class's attributes. We then add our own attribute called child_attribute to the child class.

Title of Code Sample: Creating a class for a library account with a child account for employee salaries
Objective of Code Sample: The code below provides an example of implementing inheritance in Python with a scenario related to library materials purchasing and library employee salaries.
Sample Code:

```python
class LibraryAccount:
    def __init__(self, budget):
        self.budget = budget
    def purchase(self, cost):
        if self.budget >= cost:
            self.budget -= cost
        else:
            print("Insufficient budget.")
class EmployeeAccount(LibraryAccount):
    def __init__(self, salary, budget):
        super().__init__(budget)
        self.salary = salary
    def pay_salary(self):
        self.purchase(self.salary)
employee_account = EmployeeAccount(1000, 2000)
employee_account.pay_salary()
employee_account.purchase(500)
employee_account.purchase(2000)
print(employee_account.budget)
```

In this example, we define a parent class called LibraryAccount with an init() method to initialize the budget attribute and a method to make purchases. We then define a child class called EmployeeAccount that inherits from the LibraryAccount class and adds a salary attribute and a method to pay the employee's salary by making a purchase from the budget.

We create an object called employee_account of the EmployeeAccount class with an initial budget of 2000 and a salary of 1000. We call the pay_salary() method to deduct the salary from the budget and the purchase() method to make two purchases of 500 and 2000 (the second one fails due to insufficient budget). The final print statement outputs the remaining budget, which should be 500.

POLYMORPHISM

DEFINITION OF POLYMORPHISM

Polymorphism enables a single interface to represent different types of data or objects. In the context of inheritance, polymorphism enables a subclass to inherit the methods of a parent class while also allowing the subclass to modify or override the methods as needed to suit its specific requirements.

With polymorphism, a single method can perform different actions based on the type of object it is called on. This feature enables a high degree of flexibility in the code, making it easier to maintain and extend. For instance, you might have a method named show_info that displays information about an object. If you have multiple classes that inherit from a parent class, each class can have its own implementation of the show_info method that is tailored to the particular type of object it represents.

HOW TO IMPLEMENT POLYMORPHISM IN PYTHON

In Python, polymorphism can be achieved through method overriding. Method overriding is a technique in which a subclass provides a new implementation for a method that is already defined in its parent class. The new implementation in the subclass is said to override the original implementation in the parent class. The syntax for method overriding in Python is:

```python
class ChildClass(ParentClass):
    def method_name(self, arguments):
        # New implementation for the method in the child class
```

 # Title of Code Sample: Creating a class for a library account that inherits from a main library account class and overrides certain methods
 # Objective of Code Sample: This sample code demonstrates how a class can be created that inherits from a main class.
 # Sample Code:

```python
class LibraryAccount:
    def __init__(self, budget):
        self.budget = budget
    def purchase(self, cost):
        if self.budget >= cost:
            self.budget -= cost
        else:
            print("Insufficient budget.")
    def display_balance(self):
        print(f"Remaining budget: {self.budget}")
class SpecialLibraryAccount(LibraryAccount):
    def __init__(self, budget, discount_rate):
        super().__init__(budget)
        self.discount_rate = discount_rate
    def purchase(self, cost):
```

```
        discounted_cost = cost * (1-self.discount_rate)
        if self.budget >= discounted_cost:
            self.budget -= discounted_cost
        else:
            print("Insufficient budget.")
    def display_balance(self):
        print(f"Remaining budget (special account): {self.
        budget}")
regular_account = LibraryAccount(2000)
special_account = SpecialLibraryAccount(2000, 0.1)
regular_account.purchase(1000)
special_account.purchase(1000)
regular_account.display_balance()
special_account.display_balance()
```

In this example, we define a parent class called LibraryAccount with an __init__() method to initialize the budget attribute and methods to make purchases and display the remaining balance. We then define a child class called SpecialLibraryAccount that inherits from the LibraryAccount class and adds a discount_rate attribute. The child class overrides the purchase() and display_balance() methods to provide a new implementation that takes into account the discount rate.

We create two objects, regular_account and special_account, of the LibraryAccount and SpecialLibraryAccount classes, respectively. We call the purchase() method on both objects to make a purchase of 1000, but the special account has a 10 percent discount. The display_balance() method is then called on both objects to display the remaining budget, which should be 1000 for the regular account and 1100 for the special account.

ENCAPSULATION

DEFINITION OF ENCAPSULATION

Encapsulation involves limiting access to specific parts of an object. Encapsulation encourages the grouping of data (attributes) and methods (functions) that operate on the data within a single entity called a class. Encapsulation separates concerns and enhances code modularity by preventing external interference and misuse of data. By hiding the implementation details of an object from the outside world, encapsulation makes the code more secure and less susceptible to errors.

In Python, encapsulation is achieved by making attributes and methods private or protected, meaning they can only be accessed or modified within the class or its subclasses. This is accomplished by adding a single underscore (_) or double underscore (__) before the name of the attribute or method.

Object-Oriented Programming

HOW TO IMPLEMENT ENCAPSULATION IN PYTHON

To implement encapsulation in Python, use naming conventions and property decorators. To make an attribute or method private, prefix its name with two underscores (__). To make it protected, use a single underscore (_) instead. Note that Python does not strictly enforce privacy; it's more of a convention that signals to the programmer that the attribute or method should not be accessed directly.

We can use property decorators (@property and @<attribute>.setter) to create getter and setter methods for attributes. This allows us to control the access and modification of the attribute's value.

 # Title of Code Sample: Creating a class for a library account with private attributes and methods

 # Objective of Code Sample: This code sample attests to how a class can be created that encapsulates private attributes and methods.

 # Sample Code:

```python
class LibraryAccount:
    def __init__(self, budget):
        self.__budget = budget
    @property
    def budget(self):
        return self.__budget
    @budget.setter
    def budget(self, value):
        if value >= 0:
            self.__budget = value
        else:
            print("Invalid budget value.")
    def __validate_purchase(self, cost):
        return self.__budget >= cost
    def purchase(self, cost):
        if self.__validate_purchase(cost):
            self.__budget -= cost
        else:
            print("Insufficient budget.")
    def display_balance(self):
        print(f"Remaining budget: {self.__budget}")
library_account = LibraryAccount(2000)
```

Accessing and modifying the private attribute __budget directly would result in an error

```
# library_account.__budget = 1000 # This line will cause an error
# Instead, we use the property decorator to access and modify the attribute
library_account.budget = 1000
print(library_account.budget)
library_account.purchase(500)
library_account.display_balance()
```

Attempting to call the private method __validate_purchase directly would result in an error
library_account.__validate_purchase(500) # This line will cause an error

In this example, we define a LibraryAccount class with private attributes __budget and a private method __validate_purchase(). We use property decorators to create getter and setter methods for the __budget attribute, allowing controlled access and modification. The purchase() method uses the private __validate_purchase() method to check whether there is sufficient budget for a purchase.

We create an object called library_account of the LibraryAccount class with an initial budget of 2000. We demonstrate how to use the property decorator to access and modify the private attribute __budget. Finally, we call the purchase() method to make a purchase of 500 and the display_balance() method to display the remaining budget, which should be 1500.

ABSTRACTION

DEFINITION OF ABSTRACTION

Abstraction simplifies complex systems by breaking them down into smaller, more manageable parts. It involves creating abstract classes and methods that serve as a blueprint for implementing specific functionality in concrete classes. Abstract classes are classes that can't be instantiated; they are meant to be subclassed by other classes, which must provide implementations for the abstract methods (Khoirom et al., 2020). This allows for better modularity, code reusability, and easier maintenance, as the abstract classes provide a high-level interface that encapsulates the common behavior and attributes of a group of related objects, while leaving the specific implementation details to the concrete classes.

For example, you might have an abstract class called Shape that serves as a blueprint for all types of shapes, such as squares, triangles, and circles. The Shape class might have abstract methods such as area and perimeter that represent the common behavior of all shapes, while leaving the specific implementation details to the concrete classes. By using abstraction, you can simplify complex systems, making them easier to understand and maintain.

HOW TO IMPLEMENT ABSTRACTION IN PYTHON

In Python, abstraction is achieved by using the abc module (Abstract Base Class). We can define an abstract class by inheriting from the ABC class provided by the abc module and using the @abstractmethod decorator to define abstract methods. Subclasses of an abstract class must provide concrete implementations for all its abstract methods.

#Title of Code Sample: Creating an abstract class for a library account and implementing it in specific account classes

 # Objective of Code Sample: This sample code shows how to create an abstract class and implement it in specific classes.

 # Sample Code:

```python
from abc import ABC, abstractmethod
class LibraryAccount(ABC):
    def __init__(self, budget):
        self.budget = budget
    @abstractmethod
    def purchase(self, cost):
        pass
    def display_balance(self):
        print(f"Remaining budget: {self.budget}")
class RegularLibraryAccount(LibraryAccount):
    def purchase(self, cost):
        if self.budget >= cost:
            self.budget -= cost
        else:
            print("Insufficient budget.")
class SpecialLibraryAccount(LibraryAccount):
    def __init__(self, budget, discount_rate):
        super().__init__(budget)
        self.discount_rate = discount_rate
    def purchase(self, cost):
        discounted_cost = cost * (1-self.discount_rate)
        if self.budget >= discounted_cost:
            self.budget -= discounted_cost
        else:
            print("Insufficient budget.")
regular_account = RegularLibraryAccount(2000)
special_account = SpecialLibraryAccount(2000, 0.1)
regular_account.purchase(1000)
special_account.purchase(1000)
regular_account.display_balance()
special_account.display_balance()
```

In this example, we define an abstract class called LibraryAccount that inherits from the ABC class. We declare an abstract method purchase() using the @abstractmethod decorator, which means any concrete subclass must provide an implementation for this method. The display_balance() method is a concrete method that can be used directly by subclasses.

We then define two concrete classes, RegularLibraryAccount and SpecialLibraryAccount, which inherit from the LibraryAccount abstract class and provide their own implementations for the purchase() method. The RegularLibraryAccount class implements the method without any modifications, while the SpecialLibraryAccount class adds a discount_rate attribute and modifies the purchase() method to apply the discount.

We create two objects, regular_account and special_account, of the RegularLibraryAccount and SpecialLibraryAccount classes, respectively. We call the purchase() method on both objects to make a purchase of 1000, but the special account has a 10 percent discount. The display_balance() method is then called on both objects to display the remaining budget, which should be 1000 for the regular account and 1100 for the special account.

COMPOSITION

DEFINITION OF COMPOSITION

Composition is a programming concept where we create more complex objects by combining simpler ones. It works by having one class contain instances of other classes as its attributes. This allows each class to focus on its own job while still being able to interact with other classes. Composition is often used instead of inheritance when one class "has-a" relationship with another class, rather than "is-a."

HOW TO IMPLEMENT COMPOSITION IN PYTHON

To implement composition in Python, you can define a class that includes instances of other classes as attributes. This can be achieved by initializing these instances within the class's __init__() method or by passing them as arguments when creating an instance of the class.

Title of Code Sample: Creating a class for a library and using composition to include multiple account objects
Objective of Code Sample: Here, the example code shows how to use composition to include multiple objects within a class.
Sample Code:

```
class LibraryAccount:
    def __init__(self, budget):
        self.budget = budget
```

```python
    def purchase(self, cost):
        if self.budget >= cost:
            self.budget -= cost
        else:
            print("Insufficient budget.")
    def display_balance(self):
        print(f"Remaining budget: {self.budget}")
class Library:
    def __init__(self, regular_account, special_account):
        self.regular_account = regular_account
        self.special_account = special_account
    def make_purchase(self, cost, account_type):
        if account_type == "regular":
            self.regular_account.purchase(cost)
        elif account_type == "special":
            self.special_account.purchase(cost)
        else:
            print("Invalid account type.")
    def display_balances(self):
        print("Regular account:")
        self.regular_account.display_balance()
        print("Special account:")
        self.special_account.display_balance()
regular_account = LibraryAccount(2000)
special_account = LibraryAccount(3000)
library = Library(regular_account, special_account)
library.make_purchase(1000, "regular")
library.make_purchase(1500, "special")
library.display_balances()
```

In this example, we first define a LibraryAccount class with a budget attribute and methods to make purchases and display the remaining balance. We then create a Library class that uses composition to include multiple LibraryAccount objects as attributes: regular_account and special_account.

We create two instances of the LibraryAccount class, regular_account and special_account, with initial budgets of 2000 and 3000, respectively. We then create an instance of the Library class, passing the two LibraryAccount instances as arguments.

We use the make_purchase() method of the Library class to make purchases from the regular and special accounts. Finally, we call the display_balances() method to display the remaining budgets for both accounts, which should be 1000 for the regular account and 1500 for the special account.

In this chapter, we have examined the fundamental concepts and principles of Object-Oriented Programming (OOP) in Python. OOP is a potent programming paradigm that empowers developers to generate modular, reusable, and maintainable code by organizing it into classes and objects (Budd, 2008). It enables us to model real-world entities, simplifying the development of intricate software. By comprehending and utilizing these OOP principles in Python, you can build efficient, structured, and scalable code that is more understandable, maintainable, and extensible. This approach leads to more effective software development and better overall software quality. With these principles of OOP in mind, we can move forward with working with various types of data within the Python framework.

REFERENCES

Budd, T. (2008). *Introduction to object-oriented programming*. Pearson.

Cox, B. J. (1986). *Object-oriented programming: An evolutionary approach*. Addison-Wesley Longman Publishing.

Khoirom, S., Sonia, M., Laikhuram, B., Laishram, J., & Singh, T. D. (2020). Comparative analysis of Python and Java for beginners. *International Research Journal of Engineering Technology, 7*(8), 4384–407.

Lutz, M. (2010). *Programming Python: Powerful object-oriented programming*. O'Reilly Media.

Oliphant, T. E. (2007). Python for scientific computing. *Computing in Science and Engineering, 9*(3), 10–20.

Sanner, M. F. (1999). Python: A programming language for software integration and development. *Journal of Molecular Graph Modeling, 17*(1), 57–61.

3
Data Types, Structures, Sets, and Algorithms

Data types in Python programming refer to the different categories of data supported by the language. Python supports multiple data types, including numeric, sequence, mapping, and set data types (Shein, 2015). Before we delve into the specifics of data types, it's important to understand that when you write a Python program, you are primarily working with data—receiving, sending, and manipulating it. In fact, every piece of Python code involves handling data. When you create a variable to store a value or define a function to perform an algorithm or manipulate data, you are dealing with data. Therefore, it is crucial to comprehend the different types of data, the concepts related to data manipulation, and how to handle them effectively in Python.

Data types in Python are built-in features of the language, which means you generally don't need to create your own data types from scratch to use them. Because everything in Python is an object, as Python is an Object-Oriented Programming (OOP) language, the data types in Python serve as templates that can be used to create copies with the same features and functions. To use a data type in Python, you need to define or declare it and initialize it with a value or nothing before using it. Most data types in Python are considered primitive, as they are default and fundamental data types from which other data types can be constructed. However, there are also non-primitive data types, which store values or collections of values in various formats. An example of a non-primitive data type would be creating your own Python class that stores and manipulates data. Instances of this class become data types when they are reused to solve problems. Python data types can hold numeric values, strings (combinations of numbers and letters), lists of numeric values or strings, or pairs of either.

Numeric data types include integers, floats, and complex numbers, while sequence data types consist of lists, tuples, and ranges. Dictionaries represent mapping data types, and sets represent set data types. Understanding the various data types in Python is crucial for developing efficient and effective code. Data structures, such as lists and dictionaries, enable the organization and manipulation of data in specific ways (McKinney, 2010). Algorithms, on the other hand, provide step-by-step procedures for problem-solving and can be implemented using various data structures.

In this chapter, we will delve into each data type in detail, exploring their properties and methods. We will also discuss data structures and algorithms, including arrays, linked lists, stacks, queues, trees, and graphs. Finally, the chapter will conclude with a discussion of time and space complexity and how it can be used to evaluate algorithm efficiency.

DATA TYPES

BASIC DATA TYPES IN PYTHON

In Python, there are several basic data types (primitive data types) that are used to represent different types of information (Shein, 2015). These include:

1. Integers: used to represent whole numbers. They can be positive, negative, or zero, and they can be represented in decimal (base 10), binary (base 2), octal (base 8), or hexadecimal (base 16) formats. For example, the decimal integer 10, the binary integer 0b1010, the octal integer 0o12, and the hexadecimal integer 0xA all represent the same number.
2. Floats: used to represent real numbers with a decimal point. They can be positive, negative, or zero, and they are represented in floating-point format, which allows for a tradeoff between precision and range. For example, the float 3.14 represents the value pi to two decimal places.
3. Strings: used to represent sequences of characters. They can be represented using single quotes ('), double quotes ("), or triple quotes (''' or """), and they can contain any combination of letters, numbers, punctuation, or special characters. For example, the string "Hello, World!" represents the classic introductory message in computer programming.
4. Booleans: used to represent binary values (True or False). They are often used in control flow statements to make decisions based on the truth or falsity of a particular condition. For example, the boolean expression 10 > 5 evaluates to True, while the boolean expression 10 < 5 evaluates to False.

ADVANCED DATA TYPES (NON-PRIMITIVE DATA TYPES)

In addition to the basic data types, there are also more advanced data types in Python that can be used to represent more complex information. These include:

1. Lists: a collection of ordered items that can be of any data type. Lists are represented using square brackets ([]), and individual items are separated

by commas. For example, the list [1, 2, 3, 4, 5] represents the first five positive integers. Lists are mutable, which means that the items they contain can be changed after they are created.
2. Tuples: similar to lists, but they are immutable (cannot be changed once created). Tuples are represented using parentheses (()), and individual items are separated by commas. For example, the tuple (1, 2, 3) represents a simple sequence of three numbers. Tuples are often used to represent a fixed number of related values, such as a point in two-dimensional space, or values that should not be changed in the code during execution.
3. Dictionaries: a collection of key-value pairs, where each key is associated with a specific value. Dictionaries are represented using curly braces ({}), and individual key-value pairs are separated by commas. For example, the dictionary {'name': 'John', 'age': 30, 'gender': 'male'} represents a simple profile of a person with three attributes. Dictionaries are often used to represent a collection of related values, where each value is associated with a specific label or identifier.

Title of Code Sample: Using different data types to represent a library lending account
Objective of Code Sample: This sample code describes an example that shows how we can use different data types in Python to represent a library lending account.
Sample Code:

```
# Representing a library lending account
# Integer data type to represent the account number
account_number = 123456
# String data type to represent the account holder's name
name = "John Doe"
# List data type to represent the books currently checked out
checked_out_books = ["The Great Gatsby", "To Kill a Mockingbird", "Pride and Prejudice"]
# Dictionary data type to represent the due dates for each book
due_dates = {"The Great Gatsby": "2023-07-01",
        "To Kill a Mockingbird": "2023-07-15",
        "Pride and Prejudice": "2023-07-31"}
# Boolean data type to represent whether the account is in good standing or not
good_standing = True
```

This code sample demonstrates how different data types can be used to represent real-world information in a structured and organized manner.

DATA STRUCTURES

COMPARISON OF DATA STRUCTURES IN TERMS OF USE CASES AND PERFORMANCE

Data structures are essential components of computer algorithms, used to organize and store data in a manner that makes it easier to retrieve, manipulate, and analyze. Python provides several built-in data structures, including lists, tuples, dictionaries, and sets, that are commonly used in programming (Baka, 2017).

When selecting a data structure, it's important to consider both the intended use case and the performance characteristics of each structure. For instance, lists are suitable for preserving a specific order of items and performing changes to the list, while tuples are best suited for representing collections of unchangeable items. Dictionaries are optimized for lookups based on keys, making them ideal for counting items or grouping data. Sets are beneficial for determining whether an item is present in a collection or performing set operations like union and intersection.

In terms of performance, the time complexity of each data structure is a critical consideration. For example, lists have a time complexity of O(n) for inserting an item at the start of the list but O(1) for inserting an item at the end. Dictionaries, on the other hand, have a time complexity of O(1) for both inserting and searching for items based on keys.

Choosing the appropriate data structure for the task at hand is crucial, as it can significantly impact the performance and efficiency of your code. Additionally, being familiar with the various data structures and their use cases enables you to make informed decisions about which data structure to use in a given scenario.

 # Title of Code Sample: Using different data structures to represent a list of library lending accounts
 # Objective of Code Sample: This code sample describes how different data types can be used in Python. Observe how this code sample illustrates how different data structures can be used to represent a list of library lending accounts.
 # Sample Code:

```
# Representing a list of library lending accounts
# List data type to represent the collection of accounts

accounts = [
    {"account_number": 123456, "name": "John Doe", "checked_out_books": ["The Great Gatsby", "To Kill a
```

```
Mockingbird"], "due_dates": {"The Great Gatsby": "2022-
07-01", "To Kill a Mockingbird": "2022-07-15"}, "good_
standing": True},
    {"account_number": 654321, "name": "Jane Doe",
"checked_out_books": ["Pride and Prejudice"], "due_
dates": {"Pride and Prejudice": "2022-07-31"}, "good_
standing": False}
]
```

Set data type to represent the set of books checked out across all accounts

```
checked_out_books_set = set ()
for account in accounts:
    checked_out_books_set |= set(account["checked_out_
    books"])
```

In this code sample, we use a list to represent the collection of library lending accounts, with each account represented as a dictionary. We also use a set to represent the set of books checked out across all accounts, making it easy to perform set operations such as union and intersection.

SETS

OVERVIEW OF SETS IN PYTHON

Sets are data structures in Python that are used to store a collection of unique items. They are implemented using the set type and can be created using either curly braces or the set () function. Sets are unordered, which means that the items within a set have no specific order.

One of the key features of sets is that they only allow unique items. This means that if you try to add an item to a set that already exists in the set, it will not be added again. This makes sets useful for tasks such as removing duplicates from a collection or checking whether an item is present in a collection. Sets are also optimized for membership tests, with a time complexity of O(1). This means that checking whether an item is in a set is very fast, even for large sets.

HOW TO USE SETS TO PERFORM OPERATIONS SUCH AS UNION, INTERSECTION, DIFFERENCE

Sets provide several useful operations that can be used to manipulate the items they contain. These operations include:

1. **The union operation:** combines two sets to create a new set that contains all the items from both sets. This operation is useful when you need to

merge two sets into a single set and preserve the uniqueness of the items. For example, you can use the union operation to combine two sets of library books to create a single set of all the books in both libraries.
2. **The intersection operation:** creates a new set that contains only the items that are present in both sets. This operation is useful when you need to find the items that are common to two sets. For example, you can use the intersection operation to find the books that are present in both libraries.
3. **The difference operation:** creates a new set that contains the items that are present in one set but not in another. This operation is useful when you need to find the items that are unique to one set. For example, you can use the difference operation to find the books that are only present in one library and not in the other.

Title of Code Sample: Using sets to find unique values in a list of library lending accounts
Objective of Code Sample: This example demonstrates how sets can be used to find unique values in a list of library lending accounts.
#Sample Code:

Representing a list of library lending accounts

```
accounts = [
{"account_number": 123456, "name": "John Doe", "checked_out_books": ["The Great Gatsby", "To Kill a Mockingbird"], "due_dates": {"The Great Gatsby": "2022-07-01", "To Kill a Mockingbird": "2022-07-15"}, "good_standing": True},
{"account_number": 654321, "name": "Jane Doe", "checked_out_books": ["Pride and Prejudice"], "due_dates": {"Pride and Prejudice": "2022-07-31"}, "good_standing": False}
]
```

Using a set to find the unique books checked out across all accounts

```
checked_out_books = set()
for account in accounts:
    checked_out_books |= set(account["checked_out_books"])
unique_books = list(checked_out_books)
```

In this code sample, we use a set to find the unique books checked out across all accounts. We iterate over the list of accounts, adding each set of checked-out books to the checked_out_books set using the union operation. Finally, we convert the checked_out_books set to a list to obtain a list of unique books.

ALGORITHMS

OVERVIEW OF COMMON ALGORITHMS IN PYTHON

Algorithms are a step-by-step procedure for solving problems, and there are several common algorithms in Python that are used to perform various tasks. Some of the most common algorithms in Python include:

- Sorting: used to order a collection of items in a specific way.
- Searching: used to find a specific item in a collection.
- Recursion: a technique where a function calls itself to solve a problem.

In addition, there are other, more complex or rare algorithms that you might encounter, including:

- Graph algorithms: used to process and analyze graph structures, such as finding the shortest path between two nodes.
- Dynamic programming: a technique used to solve problems by breaking them down into smaller, overlapping subproblems.
- Divide and conquer: a technique used to solve problems by dividing the problem into smaller subproblems and solving each one individually.
- Greedy algorithms: techniques used to solve problems by making the best choice at each step, without considering the long-term impact of the choices made.
- Brute force algorithms: a technique used to solve problems by trying every possible solution and choosing the best one.

These algorithms provide a range of approaches for solving problems, and the choice of algorithm will depend on the specific problem being solved and the desired performance characteristics.

TIME AND SPACE COMPLEXITY

When coding in Python, we do not only want our code to run successfully, but we also care about what time it takes for the code to run, and how much workload the computer needs to process in order to execute the code successfully. Therefore, when we talk about time and space complexity, we are referring to the efficiency of the code and the impact of the performance. When analyzing algorithms, it is important to consider both the time and space complexity, as these factors can greatly impact the overall performance of the solution. Therefore, time complexity refers to the amount of time an algorithm takes to run as a function of the size of the input. It is often expressed using the "big O" notation, which provides an upper bound on the running time of the algorithm. This can help to identify the most time-consuming parts of an algorithm and determine whether it will be able to handle large inputs in a reasonable amount of time. Think of it as a way of measuring how long it will take for the code to execute—from when it's been run, compiled, to the moment it gets executed.

Space complexity refers to the amount of memory an algorithm uses as a function of the size of the input. Like time complexity, space complexity is also expressed using the "big O" notation, and it provides an upper bound on the memory usage of the algorithm. It is important to consider space complexity because memory constraints can limit the scalability of a solution and impact its overall performance. By considering both time and space complexity, developers can make informed decisions about which algorithms to use for specific tasks and optimize the performance of their code.

Title of Code Sample: Using algorithms to sort a list of library lending accounts by number of materials lent
Objective of Code Sample: This sample code shows how an algorithm can be used to sort library lending accounts.
Sample Code:

Representing a list of library lending accounts

```
accounts = [
    {"account_number": 123456, "name": "John Doe", "checked_out_books": ["The Great Gatsby", "To Kill a Mockingbird"], "due_dates": {"The Great Gatsby": "2022-07-01", "To Kill a Mockingbird": "2022-07-15"}, "good_standing": True},
    {"account_number": 654321, "name": "Jane Doe", "checked_out_books": ["Pride and Prejudice"], "due_dates": {"Pride and Prejudice": "2022-07-31"}, "good_standing": False}
]
```

Using a sorting algorithm to sort the accounts by the number of materials lent

```
accounts.sort(key=lambda x: len(x["checked_out_books"]), reverse=True)
```

In this code sample, we use the sorting function in Python, which implements a sorting algorithm, to sort the list of library lending accounts by the number of materials lent. The key argument is used to specify the function that should be used for sorting, in this case the lambda function feed with the length of the checked_out_books list. The reverse argument is used to specify whether the list should be sorted in reverse order.

The above code sample will save lots of time and reduce the space or workload on the computer processing power, because it puts into accounts a smarter way of handling sorting-related issues other than the traditional looping through of a list of items, which takes longer time to complete and creates more workload to be processed.

This chapter has provided an exploration of data types, data structures, sets, and algorithms in Python. By understanding the different data types and their properties, developers can choose the appropriate data structure for their use case and optimize the performance of their code. Additionally, understanding data structures and algorithms allows developers to organize and manipulate data efficiently, leading to more effective problem-solving. This information serves as a building block for our discussion of functions in the next chapter. Together these chapters serve as the backbone of our discussion of the Python language.

REFERENCES

Baka, B. (2017). *Python data structures and algorithms*. Packt Publishing.

McKinney, W. (2010). Data structures for statistical computing in Python. *Proceedings of the 9th Python in Science Conference, 445*, 51–56.

Shein, E. (2015). Python for beginners. *Communication of the ACM, 58*(3), 19–21.

4

Functions

CODE THAT PUTS OUR DATA TO WORK

In this chapter, we will delve into the topic of functions in Python. Here, we explore the importance of functions in code organization and reusability. Functions are a crucial aspect of programming, allowing developers to write reusable code that can be easily maintained and scaled (Bassi, 2007). In this chapter, we will begin with a brief overview of functions in Python and their importance, followed by a comprehensive discussion of how to define and call functions, as well as the syntax for doing so. The chapter will then explore the concept of function scope, including the LEGB rule, which defines the order in which variables are searched when a function is called. The different types of function arguments, including positional, keyword, and default arguments, will also be discussed, along with the use of *args and **kwargs to handle variable-length argument lists. Recursion and lambda functions will also be covered, with a discussion of when and how to use these advanced features of functions in Python.

WHAT IS FUNCTION IN PYTHON?

In Python, as well as in most programming languages, functions are blocks of code that help solve problems. Think of them as formulas you use when solving mathematical problems. Unlike in math, you have the freedom to define your own functions. Some functions are predefined, meaning they come with the Python programming language, while others can be custom-defined by you for your specific use.

It is important to note that you do not need to write another function if one already exists for your needs. So, how can you determine whether a function you need already exists in Python? The Python official documentation is the right place to start looking when you're unsure whether a function already exists for the problem you're trying to solve. At the time this book was written, the official web link to the Python documentation on functions could be found here: https://docs.python.org/3/glossary.html#term-function. You can also find this link by searching "Python function" in any search engine.

Let's say you want to write a function that searches through collections of books to find those with a specific word in their titles and provides a list of matching books. How can you determine whether there is already a function available in Python to accomplish this task? Simply search the Python documentation website page to identify the appropriate function. This task can be achieved using the search and sorting functions that are already predefined in Python. To use a function, whether predefined by Python or custom-defined by you, you need to call it in your code.

DEFINING AND CALLING FUNCTIONS

SYNTAX FOR DEFINING AND CALLING FUNCTIONS IN PYTHON

In Python, functions are defined using the "def" keyword, followed by the function name and a set of parentheses that may contain arguments. Functions can be called by using the function name followed by a set of parentheses that may contain arguments. For example, the following syntax will allow you to define a function in Python:

```
def function_name(arg1, arg2, ...):
  # function body
  # statements
  return value
```

And this example code will allow you to call the function:

```
def greet(name):
  print("Hello, " + name + "!")
greet("John") # Output: Hello, John!
```

FUNCTION ARGUMENTS AND RETURN VALUES

Function arguments are values or expressions that are passed to a function when it is called. These arguments can be used within the function to perform specific operations or calculations. Function arguments can be positional, meaning that they are passed in a specific order, or they can be keyword arguments, meaning that they are passed by name (Bassi, 2007).

The *return value* of a function is specified using the return statement. The value or expression following the return keyword is the value that is returned to the caller of the function. The return value can be used by the caller to perform additional operations or store the result of the function.

When a function is called, it is executed from start to finish (Dobesova, 2011). The function arguments are processed, and any operations within the function body are performed. The function can use the arguments passed to it to perform specific calculations, and it can also return a value to the caller. The execution of the function ends when a return statement is encountered or the end of the function is reached.

Title of Code Sample: Python function to calculate the average number of books borrowed by library patrons
Objective of Code Sample: This code sample shows how to use some basic calculations for the library—like finding the average number of books borrowed.
Sample Code:

```
def average_books_borrowed(patrons):
    total = 0
    for patron in patrons:
        total += len(patron["checked_out_books"])
    return total / len(patrons)
```

Call the function with a list of library patrons

```
library_patrons = [{"checked_out_books": ["Book 1", "Book 2"]},
          {"checked_out_books": ["Book 3", "Book 4", "Book 5"]},
          {"checked_out_books": ["Book 6"]}]
avg_books_borrowed = average_books_borrowed(library_patrons)
print("Average number of books borrowed:", avg_books_borrowed)
```

In this code sample, the function "average_books_borrowed" takes a list of library patrons as its argument and calculates the average number of books borrowed by summing the number of books borrowed by each patron and dividing by the number of patrons. The function is then called with a list of library patrons, and the result is printed to the console.

FUNCTION SCOPE

OVERVIEW OF LOCAL AND GLOBAL SCOPE IN FUNCTIONS

Function scope refers to the visibility and accessibility of variables within a function (Politz et al., 2013). In other words, it determines which variables can be used and modified within a function, and which variables can be used outside the function. There are two main types of scope in functions: local scope and global scope.

Local scope refers to variables that are declared and used within a function. These variables are only accessible and usable within the function in which they are declared. Local variables are created every time a function is called and are destroyed after the function returns.

Global scope refers to variables that are declared outside of any function and can be accessed and used by any function in the program. Global variables persist throughout the lifetime of the program and can be modified by any function.

It is important to understand the difference between local and global scope in functions as they can affect the behavior and efficiency of your code. In general, it is recommended to use local variables whenever possible, as they help to limit the scope of the variables, which makes the code easier to understand and maintain. Global variables, on the other hand, should be used sparingly, as they can cause unexpected behavior and make the code harder to debug. When accessing global variables within a function, it is necessary to use the global keyword to indicate that you want to access the global variable and not create a local variable with the same name.

THE LEGB RULE (LOCAL, ENCLOSING, GLOBAL, BUILT-IN)

The LEGB rule (local, enclosing, global, built-in) is a mnemonic that helps developers remember the order in which Python searches for variables (Unpingco, 2021). It states that Python searches for a variable in the following order:

1. Local scope
2. Enclosing scope (the scope of any enclosing function)
3. Global scope
4. Built-in scope (Python's built-in functions and variables)

The LEGB rule is an important concept in understanding the scope of variables in Python. When a variable is referenced within a function, Python first looks for the variable in the local scope, which includes all variables declared within the current function. If the variable is not found in the local scope, Python then looks in the enclosing scope, which includes any variables declared in any enclosing functions. If the variable is still not found, Python then checks the global scope, which includes all variables declared outside of any function in the program. Finally, if the variable is not found in the global scope, Python checks the built-in scope, which includes all built-in functions and variables in Python. Understanding the LEGB rule is crucial in avoiding scope-related errors and ensuring that your program is working as expected.

Title of Code Sample: Functions and global variables: include global variable in functions
Objective of Code Sample: This code sample illustrates how to use a global variable within a function to keep track of the total number of books borrowed from a library.
Sample Code:

Global variable to keep track of the total number of books borrowed from the library

```
total_books_borrowed = 0
def borrow_book(number_of_books):
```

Access the global variable

```
global total_books_borrowed
```

Add the number of books borrowed to the total

```
total_books_borrowed += number_of_books
```

Return the updated total

```
return total_books_borrowed
```

Call the function and print the result

```
print(borrow_book(2))  # 2
print(borrow_book(3))  # 5
```

In this example, the global variable total_books_borrowed is used to keep track of the total number of books borrowed from the library. The borrow_book function accesses the global variable and adds the number of books passed as an argument to the total. The updated total is then returned and printed.

FUNCTION ARGUMENTS

OVERVIEW OF DIFFERENT TYPES OF FUNCTION ARGUMENTS

Function arguments are the values that are passed to a function when it is called. There are several types of function arguments, including:

1. **Positional arguments:** These are the simplest type of function arguments. They are assigned to function parameters based on the position in which they are passed. For example, if you have a function with two parameters, the first argument passed to the function will be assigned to the first parameter, and the second argument will be assigned to the second parameter.

2. **Keyword arguments:** These are function arguments that are assigned to function parameters using the parameter name. Keyword arguments allow you to specify arguments in any order, as long as you use the parameter name. For example, you could call a function with the first argument passed as a keyword argument, and the second argument passed as a positional argument.
3. **Default arguments:** These are function arguments that have a default value if no value is passed to the function. This can be useful in cases where a function is frequently called with the same argument, or if a default value makes sense for the function. For example, you could have a default argument for the number of items to return in a list, with a default value of 10.
4. **Variable-length arguments:** These are function arguments that allow you to pass a variable number of arguments to a function. There are two types of variable-length arguments in Python: *args and **kwargs. *args allows you to pass a variable number of positional arguments to a function, while **kwargs allows you to pass a variable number of keyword arguments. These types of arguments can be useful when you want to write a flexible function that can handle a varying number of arguments.

*HOW TO USE *ARGS AND **KWARGS TO HANDLE VARIABLE-LENGTH ARGUMENT LISTS*

To handle variable-length argument lists, you can use the *args and **kwargs syntax. When using *args, you can pass any number of non-keyword arguments to a function. The arguments are passed to the function as a tuple. To use args, you simply add an asterisk () followed by the argument name in the function definition. For example:

```
def func(*args):
  for arg in args:
    print(arg)
func(1, 2, 3, 4)
```

In this example, the function func() takes any number of non-keyword arguments and prints each of them.

Similarly, to use **kwargs, you can pass any number of keyword arguments to a function. The keyword arguments are passed to the function as a dictionary. To use kwargs, you add two asterisks () followed by the argument name in the function definition. For example:

```
def func(**kwargs):
  for key, value in kwargs.items():
    print(key, value)
func(a=1, b=2, c=3)
```

In this example, the function func() takes any number of keyword arguments and prints each of them. Note that kwargs is a conventional name for keyword arguments, but you can use any name you like.

Title of Code Sample: Creating functions for processing any number of library accounts
Objective of Code Sample: With this example code, we demonstrate how to use *args and **kwargs to handle a variable-length argument list.
Sample Code:

```
def process_library_accounts(*accounts, **details):
    for account in accounts:
      print("Processing account:", account)
    for key, value in details.items():
      print(f"{key}: {value}")
```

Call the function with a variable number of arguments

```
process_library_accounts("John Doe", "Jane Doe", "Jim Smith", library="Library A", location="New York")
```

Output:
Processing account: John Doe
Processing account: Jane Doe
Processing account: Jim Smith
library: Library A
location: New York

In this example, the process_library_accounts function takes any number of library accounts as *accounts and processes them. The function also takes any number of keyword arguments as **details. The function iterates over the accounts and details and prints them.

RECURSION

OVERVIEW OF RECURSION IN FUNCTIONS

Recursion is a powerful technique in programming that allows for a modular and organized approach to problem-solving (Downey, 2012). It is especially useful for solving problems that can be broken down into smaller, simpler sub-problems. By calling the same function repeatedly, recursion can solve a problem by solving smaller instances of the same problem.

When using recursion, it's important to ensure that the function has a base case, which is the condition that will cause the function to stop calling itself recursively. Without a base case, the function will continue to call itself indefinitely, resulting in a stack overflow error.

Recursive functions can be challenging to design and debug, but they can lead to elegant and efficient code. In Python, recursion can be used to solve problems such as searching and sorting, tree traversal, and mathematical computations such as factorial and Fibonacci sequences.

To use recursion effectively, it's important to understand the problem and determine how it can be broken down into smaller sub-problems. The recursive function should then be designed to solve the base case and make a recursive call to solve the sub-problem. By breaking the problem down into smaller parts, recursion can simplify complex problems and lead to more organized and maintainable code.

 # Title of Code Sample: Creating a recursive function for calculating the factorial of a number
 # Objective of Code Sample: This code sample shows how to use recursion to calculate the factorial of a number.
 # Sample Code:

```
def factorial(n):
    # Base case
        if n == 0:
        return 1
    # Recursive case
        return n * factorial(n-1)
    # Call the function and print the result
        print(factorial(5))  # 120
```

In this example, the factorial function takes a single argument n and returns the factorial of n. The function has a base case that stops the recursion when n is equal to 0. The base case returns 1, which is the result of 0! (the factorial of 0). The recursive case calculates the factorial of n by multiplying n by the result of the factorial function called with n-1. This process continues until the base case is reached.

LAMBDA FUNCTIONS

OVERVIEW OF LAMBDA FUNCTIONS IN PYTHON

Lambda functions are a powerful and concise way to create small, one-time-use functions in Python (Dubois et al., 1996). They are commonly used in functional programming, and can be passed as arguments to higher-order functions such as map(), filter(), and reduce(). In addition, lambda functions can be used to create simple functions that are used as the key function in sorting operations, or as short, throwaway functions that are used only once.

Lambda functions have a more compact syntax than regular functions, allowing you to define a function in a single line. However, they are limited in scope, can only contain a single expression, and cannot contain statements or annotations. Despite these limitations, they can still be incredibly useful in simplifying code and improving its readability.

When using lambda functions, it's important to keep their limitations in mind and to use them appropriately. In general, lambda functions are best used for simple tasks or as part of larger functional programming constructs. By using lambda functions effectively, you can create code that is more concise, more readable, and easier to maintain.

Title of Code Sample: Creating a lambda function to sort a list of library accounts by number of books borrowed
Objective of Code Sample: This code example shows how to use a lambda function to sort a list of library accounts by the number of books borrowed.
Sample Code:

```
library_accounts = [
{"name": "John Doe", "books_borrowed": 5},
{"name": "Jane Doe", "books_borrowed": 2},
{"name": "Jim Smith", "books_borrowed": 3},
]
```

Use a lambda function to sort the list of library accounts by the number of books borrowed

```
sorted_library_accounts = sorted(library_accounts,
key=lambda x: x["books_borrowed"])
```

Print the sorted list of library accounts

```
for account in sorted_library_accounts:
print(account["name"], account["books_borrowed"])
```

Output:
Jane Doe 2
Jim Smith 3
John Doe 5

In this example, the sorted function takes a list of library accounts and sorts it based on the number of books borrowed. The lambda function lambda x: x["books_borrowed"] is passed as the key argument to the sorted function. The lambda function takes a single argument x and returns the value of the

Functions

books_borrowed key. The sorted function uses the result of the lambda function as the sorting key and returns the sorted list of library accounts.

This chapter covered the fundamentals of functions in Python, including their importance in code organization and reusability. We examined the syntax and structure of functions, as well as the concept of function scope and how it impacts variable access. The different types of function arguments, as well as variable-length argument lists, were also discussed in detail. Additionally, we explored recursion and lambda functions and their use cases in Python. With this knowledge, we have acquired the necessary background to proceed with using Python for addressing many of the significant issues we face in libraries and information organizations today.

REFERENCES

Bassi, S. (2007). A primer on Python for life science researchers. *PLoS Computational Biology, 3*(11), e199.

Dobesova, Z. (2011). Programming language Python for data processing. *International Conference on Electrical and Control Engineering, 2011,* 4866-69.

Downey, A. (2012). *Think Python.* O'Reilly Media.

Dubois, P. F., Hinsen, K., & Hugunin, J. (1996). Numerical Python. *Computers in Physics, 10*(3), 262-67.

Politz, J. G., et al. (2013). Python: The full monty. *ACM SIGPLAN Notices, 48*(10), 217-32.

Unpingco, J. (2021). *Python programming for data analysis.* Springer.

5
Importing, Creating, and Maintaining Data Files

Welcome to chapter 5, in which we will explore the topic of importing, creating, and maintaining data files in Python. Data files are a critical component of many software applications, and it is essential for us to know how to handle them effectively. This chapter will cover the various file formats commonly used for data storage and how to import them into Python using libraries and modules. We will also discuss the process of creating data files and the best practices for maintaining them.

There are various scenarios in which importing or exporting files becomes necessary when writing a software program in Python. Libraries and similar organizations deal with significant amounts of data, both transactional and historical. Transactional data covers day-to-day activities, while historical data helps document how things are done within the organization. Therefore, having a good understanding of how to handle data files in Python is essential to meet the needs of both the clientele and the organization.

Let's consider an example to illustrate the importance of data files when writing a Python program. Imagine you have a single file containing a list of books along with their descriptions. The library administrator requests that you check the list to ensure it does not contain certain titles or categories of resources that the board of trustees has agreed should not be in the library. If the list contains thousands of titles, manually sorting through each one to meet the requirement would be time-consuming. Even using functions in a spreadsheet application would still take considerable time. It becomes impractical to repeatedly perform the same manual task when a few lines of code could handle it efficiently.

Therefore, utilizing data files in Python becomes incredibly useful when dealing with large datasets that require manipulation or transformation.

However, before importing a data file into your Python code, it is crucial to understand the task requirements. Understanding these requirements guides the decision-making process of which parts of the file, such as fields, should be considered and which should be excluded. This selection criteria typically occurs during data preprocessing and cleaning of the dataset. In subsequent sections of this book, we will explore use cases and sample Python codes that involve data transformation and discuss how data preprocessing is performed.

It is important to note that whenever data files are used in Python code, understanding the specific requirements for using them is paramount. This understanding determines the appropriate transformation of the data, including the necessary fields for carrying out the task. The same consideration applies when contemplating the export of a dataset from within your code.

IMPORTING DATA FILES

Data files are computer files that contain data in various formats. They serve as repositories for storing and retrieving data, facilitating data exchange, transforming data types, providing interpretive parameters for data formatting, and logging data activity. For instance, a Word file stores document data, an email attachment allows data to be shared across different locations, and converting data from one type to another is a form of data transformation. Additionally, data files can include information about when they were last edited.

OVERVIEW OF DIFFERENT FILE FORMATS

When working with data, there are numerous formats available for storing and importing data. You may already be familiar with file formats such as Word documents, Excel spreadsheets, and PowerPoint presentations. In Python, there are several file formats commonly used for storing and importing data (van Rossum, 2007). Some of the most frequently encountered file formats include:

- CSV (Comma-Separated Values): This is a plain text file format that stores data in a tabular form, with each row representing a record and each column representing a field. The values in each row are separated by commas. Example: a CSV file containing a library catalog with columns for book titles, authors, publication dates, and genres.
- Excel: This is a proprietary file format used by Microsoft Excel. It stores data in a spreadsheet form, with each sheet representing a table and each row and column representing a record and a field, respectively. Example: an Excel file containing library circulation data with sheets for different years, where each row represents a borrower and each column represents a book checkout.

- JSON (JavaScript Object Notation): This is a text-based data format that is used to store and exchange data. JSON data is structured as a collection of key-value pairs and can be used to represent complex data structures. Example: a JSON file containing library patron information, where each key-value pair represents a specific attribute such as name, address, and membership status.
- TXT: This is a plain text file format that stores data as plain text, with each line of the file representing a record. Example: a TXT file containing a library event log, where each line represents an event such as book returns, reservations, or system notifications.
- XML (Extensible Markup Language): This is a markup language used to store data in a treelike structure, with each element in the tree representing a different aspect of the data. Example: an XML file containing library metadata, where elements represent books, authors, genres, and related information organized hierarchically.
- Binary: This is a non-text file format that stores data in binary format. Binary files are often used for storing large amounts of data or for storing data that is not meant to be read or edited by humans. Example: a binary file containing digitized copies of library archival materials, such as scanned documents, images, or audio recordings.

In addition to these file formats, there are also specific file formats used for specific purposes, such as PDF for documents, PNG for images, and MP3 for audio files. The choice of file format will depend on the specific use case and requirements of the data being stored and imported.

Python offers a range of libraries and modules that are specifically designed for importing data files. Here are some notable ones:

1. Pandas: Pandas is a widely used library for data analysis and manipulation. It provides efficient and powerful data structures, such as DataFrames, which simplify working with structured data. With Pandas, you can seamlessly import data from formats like CSV, Excel, and JSON, and perform various data operations (McKinney, 2011).
2. Openpyxl: Openpyxl is a library dedicated to working with Excel files. It enables reading, writing, and manipulation of Excel spreadsheets using Python. With Openpyxl, you can extract data from Excel files, modify existing data, and create new sheets.
3. Numpy: Numpy is a fundamental library for numerical computing in Python. It introduces powerful data structures like arrays and matrices, along with a collection of mathematical functions. Numpy supports reading and writing data in formats like CSV and binary files, making it valuable for scientific computing tasks (Van der Walt et al., 2011).

4. Matplotlib: Matplotlib is a popular plotting library that facilitates the creation of visualizations. It offers an extensive array of plotting functions, such as line plots, scatter plots, bar plots, and histograms. Matplotlib allows you to export your plots to various file formats, including PNG, PDF, and SVG.
5. Os: The 'os' module is part of Python's standard library and provides functionalities to interact with the operating system. It assists in reading and writing files, manipulating file paths, and accessing file metadata. The 'os' module is versatile and serves as a foundation for file-related operations.
6. Csv: The 'csv' module, also part of the standard library, offers support specifically for reading and writing CSV files. It provides functions for handling CSV data, allowing you to read data from CSV files, write new data to them, and manipulate the contents as needed.

By utilizing these libraries and modules in conjunction, you can effectively import, manipulate, and visualize data in various formats. This capability empowers you to extract insights and make informed decisions based on data-driven analysis.

 # Title of Code Sample: Importing a CSV file with library account data using the Pandas library

 # Objective of Code Sample: With this code sample, we demonstrate how to use the Pandas library to import a CSV file with library account data.

 # Sample Code:

```
import pandas as pd
```

Read the CSV file into a pandas DataFrame

```
df = pd.read_csv("library_accounts.csv")
```

Print the first 5 records of the DataFrame

```
print(df.head())
```

In this example, the Pandas library is imported as pd. The read_csv function is used to read the CSV file library_accounts.csv into a Pandas DataFrame. The head function is used to print the first five records of the DataFrame. The DataFrame is a two-dimensional data structure that can be used to represent and manipulate tabular data.

CREATING DATA FILES

THE PROCESS OF CREATING FILES

The process of creating a file in Python involves opening a file, writing data to the file, and then closing the file. The data can be written in various formats, such as plain text, CSV, Excel, or JSON, depending on the requirements of the project (Langtangen, 2016).

To create a file in Python, you first need to use the open function to create a file object. The open function takes two arguments: the name of the file you want to create, and the mode in which you want to open the file (e.g., 'w' for write mode). Once you have a file object, you can write data to it using the write method. When you're done writing the file, you should close it using the close method to ensure that all data has been written to disk and to free up any resources used by the file.

For example, here is how you could create a plain text file and write some data to it:

```python
# Open a file in write mode
f = open('example.txt', 'w')
# Write some data to the file
f.write('Hello, world!')
# Close the file
f.close()
```

In this example, we first use the open function to create a file object for the file example.txt in write mode ('w'). We then write the string 'Hello, world!' to the file using the write method. Finally, we close the file using the close method. After running this code, you will have a file named example.txt in your current working directory that contains the text Hello, world!

If you want to write data to a file in a more structured format, such as CSV or JSON, you can use a library such as Pandas or the built-in csv and json modules to do so. These libraries provide convenient functions for reading and writing data in the desired format, so you don't have to manually write the code to format the data yourself.

 # Title of Code Sample: Creating a CSV file with library account data using the Pandas library
 # Objective of Code Sample: Here we provide an example of how to use the Pandas library to create a CSV file with library account data.
 # Sample Code:

```python
import pandas as pd
# Create a pandas DataFrame with library account data
library_accounts = {
"account_number": [100, 101, 102, 103, 104],
```

Importing, Creating, and Maintaining Data Files

```
"name": ["John Doe", "Jane Doe", "Jim Smith", "Sarah
Lee", "Michael J"],
"books_borrowed": [5, 2, 3, 7, 4]
}
df = pd.DataFrame(library_accounts)
```

Write the DataFrame to a CSV file

```
df.to_csv("library_accounts.csv", index=False)
```

In this example, a Pandas DataFrame is created with library account data. The DataFrame is then written to a CSV file using the to_csv function. The index argument is set to False to exclude the index column from the output file. The resulting CSV file can be easily opened and manipulated using a spreadsheet application or loaded into a Python script for further analysis.

MAINTAINING DATA FILES

OVERVIEW OF DIFFERENT WAYS TO HANDLE DATA FILE MAINTENANCE IN PYTHON

Data file maintenance is an important aspect of data management, as it ensures that the data is accurate, up-to-date, and usable. In Python, there are several ways to handle data file maintenance, including:

- Updating: This involves making changes to existing records in a data file. For example, updating the number of books borrowed for a library account.
- Deleting: This involves removing records from a data file. For example, deleting a library account that is no longer active.
- Appending: This involves adding new records to a data file. For example, adding a new library account to the existing list of accounts.

It is important to handle data file maintenance efficiently to keep the data organized and up-to-date. There are various libraries and modules available in Python that can be used for data file maintenance, such as Pandas and Openpyxl.

When using Pandas to handle data file maintenance, updating records can be done by using the loc method to locate the specific row to be updated and then updating the values in the desired columns. Deleting records can be done by using the drop method to specify the index of the row to be deleted. Appending records can be done by using the append method to add a new row to the existing DataFrame.

When using Openpyxl to handle data file maintenance, updating records can be done by using the cell method to locate the specific cell to be updated and then updating the value in that cell. Deleting records can be done by using the delete_rows method to specify the range of rows to be deleted. Appending records can be done by adding a new row to the existing worksheet.

It is important to be cautious when performing data file maintenance, as any mistakes can result in data loss or corruption. It is recommended to make a backup of the data file before making any changes.

Title of Code Sample: Updating a CSV file with library account data using the Pandas library
Objective of Code Sample: This sample code shows how the Pandas library can be used to update a CSV file with library account data.
Sample Code:

```
import pandas as pd
# Read the CSV file into a pandas DataFrame
df = pd.read_csv("library_accounts.csv")
# Update the number of books borrowed for a specific library account
df.loc[df["account_number"] == 102, "books_borrowed"] = 4
# Write the updated DataFrame to the CSV file
df.to_csv("library_accounts.csv", index=False)
```

In this example, the CSV file library_accounts.csv is read into a Pandas DataFrame using the read_csv function. The loc method is used to update the number of books borrowed for a specific library account. The updated DataFrame is then written to the CSV file using the to_csv function. The index argument is set to False to exclude the index column from the output file.

FILE HANDLING WITH OS MODULE

OS MODULE IN PYTHON

The os module in Python is a built-in module that provides a way to interact with the operating system and perform various tasks that are related to file and directory management. This module is particularly useful for managing and manipulating files and directories in a programmatic way.

Some of the most commonly used functions of the os module for file system interactions are:

- os.listdir(path): This function returns a list of files and directories in the specified path. This function can be used to get a list of all the files and directories in a directory and perform various operations on them.

Importing, Creating, and Maintaining Data Files

- os.mkdir(path): This function creates a new directory at the specified path. If the directory already exists, this function will raise a FileExistsError.
- os.rmdir(path): This function removes the specified directory at path. This function will only remove the directory if it is empty. If the directory is not empty, this function will raise an OSError.
- os.path.exists(path): This function returns True if the specified path exists and False otherwise. This function can be used to check whether a file or directory exists before performing any operations on it.
- os.path.isfile(path): This function returns True if the specified path is a file and False otherwise. This function can be used to check whether a path is a file or a directory before performing any operations on it.

 # Title of Code Sample: Using the os module to check if a specific data file exists
 # Objective of Code Sample: This sample code demonstrates how to use the os module to check whether a specific data file exists.
 # Sample Code:

```python
import os
file_path = "library_accounts.csv"
if os.path.exists(file_path):
    print(f"The file '{file_path}' exists.")
else:
    print(f"The file '{file_path}' does not exist.")
```

In this example, the os.path.exists function is used to check if the file library_accounts.csv exists. If the file exists, a message is printed indicating that the file exists. If the file does not exist, a message is printed indicating that the file does not exist.

Working with data files is an essential part of programming, and the ability to effectively import, create, and maintain data files is crucial for any developer. In this chapter, we explored different file formats and libraries that can be used to import data files into Python. We also looked at the process of creating files and different ways to handle data file maintenance in Python. Finally, we discussed the OS module and its use in file handling. With the knowledge gained from this chapter, you can confidently work with data files in your projects, leading to more efficient and effective data management.

REFERENCES

Langtangen, H. P. (2016). *A primer on scientific programming with Python*. Springer-Verlag.

McKinney, W. (2011). Pandas: A foundational Python library for data analysis and statistics. *Python for High Performance and Scientific Computing, 14*(9), 1–9.

Van der Walt, S., Colbert, S. C., & Varoquaux, G. (2011). The NumPy array: A structure for efficient numerical computation. *Computing in Science and Engineering, 13*(2), 22–30.

Van Rossum, G. (2007). Python programming language. *USENIX Annual Technical Conference, 41*(1), 1–36.

6
Testing and Troubleshooting

In chapter 6 of this guide to Python programming, we will dive into the world of testing and troubleshooting in Python. Testing is an important part of the development process, as it helps ensure that your code is functioning correctly and meets the requirements of your project (Sale, 2014). In this chapter, we will discuss the different types of testing and the best practices for designing data structures and algorithms in Python. We will additionally cover troubleshooting techniques, including an overview of common issues that arise in Python code. This should help you to diagnose and resolve problems in your code, ensuring that your projects are running smoothly. We will conclude with some discussion of profilers and their use in Python and provide tips for avoiding common pitfalls in data structure and algorithm design.

TYPES OF TESTING

DIFFERENT TYPES OF TESTING

Testing is a critical part of software development and is important for ensuring that software systems are functioning as intended (Sale, 2014). Different types of testing serve different purposes and are used to validate different aspects of a software system. There are several types of testing that can be performed in software development, including:

- Unit testing: This testing approach focuses on individual units or components of a software system, validating their functionality independently. It involves testing specific code elements, such as functions or classes (Trautsch & Grabowski, 2017).
- Integration testing: This testing method examines the interactions between different components or systems, ensuring their proper collaboration. It verifies that the various components of a system work together correctly.

- Acceptance testing: This type of testing evaluates the overall functionality of a software system. It aims to confirm that the system meets the requirements and expectations of end users.
- Functional testing: This testing technique verifies whether a software system behaves as expected in response to specific inputs and events. It covers areas such as input validation, error handling, and boundary conditions.
- Regression testing: This testing method ensures that changes made to a software system haven't introduced new bugs or caused existing functionality to break. It confirms that the system continues to work as expected after modifications.
- Performance testing: This testing approach measures the performance and scalability of a software system. It evaluates response time, throughput, and resource utilization under different load conditions.
- Security testing: This type of testing evaluates the security of a software system. It locates vulnerabilities, identifies potential threats, and assesses the effectiveness of security controls.

It is important to note that different types of testing serve different purposes and are performed at different stages of the software development process. In general, a combination of different types of testing is used to ensure that a software system is of high quality and meets the needs of its users.

WHEN TO USE EACH TYPE OF TESTING

It is important to use the right type of testing at the appropriate stage of the development process to ensure that the software is functioning correctly and meets the requirements and expectations of end users (Arbuckle, 2010):

- Unit tests are typically used early in the development process to validate individual units of code.
- Integration tests are used after the individual units have been tested to validate the interactions between different components.
- Acceptance tests are utilized near the end of the development process to validate the overall functionality of a system.
- Functional tests are typically performed during the middle stages of the development process, after the individual units of code have been tested and before the overall system is evaluated.
- Regression tests are employed after changes have been made to the software system, to ensure that the changes have not impacted the existing functionality.
- Performance tests are usually performed toward the later stages of the development process, after the system has been integrated and functional testing has been completed.

- Security tests are often used along with other types of testing, or even after the system has been deployed, to continuously evaluate the security of the system.

Title of Code Sample: Regression analysis of library resources
Objective of Code Sample: This code segment demonstrates how to use the unittest library to create a unit test for Python codes.
Sample Code:

```
import unittest
def add(a, b):
 return a + b
class TestAddition(unittest.TestCase):
 def test_addition(self):
  self.assertEqual(add(1, 2), 3)
  self.assertEqual(add(0, 0), 0)
  self.assertEqual(add(-1, -1), -2)
if __name__ == '__main__':
 unittest.main()
```

In this example, a simple add function is defined to add two numbers. A test case class TestAddition is then defined to test the add function. The unittest.TestCase class provides several methods for testing, including assertEqual, which is used to validate that the result of the add function is equal to the expected value. The test case class is executed using the unittest.main function. If all tests pass, the output will be "." for each test, indicating that the tests were successful.

TROUBLESHOOTING TECHNIQUES

AN OVERVIEW OF COMMON ISSUES THAT ARISE IN PYTHON CODE

There are several types of issues that can arise in Python code, each with its unique characteristics and implications (Kohn, 2019). Syntax errors are one common type of issue that occurs when the code does not adhere to the syntax rules of the Python language. These errors are often caused by missing parentheses, quotes, or other syntax elements. For instance, forgetting to close a parenthesis or mistyping a keyword can lead to a syntax error. When encountered, the code cannot be executed until the syntax error is fixed.

Semantic errors, on the other hand, manifest when the code is syntactically correct but fails to produce the expected results. These errors typically stem from logic errors or incorrect data types. For instance, assigning an integer value to a variable intended for string data can result in unexpected behavior. Resolving semantic errors involves analyzing the code's logic and ensuring the appropriate data types are used.

Runtime errors occur during the execution of the code and can manifest in various forms. Examples include division by zero or attempting to access an index that does not exist in a list. These errors are typically caused by unexpected conditions or exceptional circumstances that arise during program execution. Proper exception handling and debugging techniques are necessary to identify and resolve runtime errors.

Logic errors represent errors in the logic or design of the code, resulting in unintended behavior or incorrect results. They occur when the code fails to produce the expected output due to flawed logic. For instance, a conditional statement that evaluates incorrectly or a loop that terminates prematurely can introduce logic errors. Identifying and fixing logic errors often involves careful examination of the code's structure and logic flow (Kambaraliyevich, 2022).

Memory errors arise when the code utilizes more memory than is available, leading to crashes or other unexpected behavior (Redondo & Ortin, 2014). These errors commonly occur when working with large datasets or inefficient memory management. They can cause programs to slow down, freeze, or terminate unexpectedly. Memory errors require efficient memory allocation and deallocation strategies to ensure optimal memory usage.

TROUBLESHOOTING TECHNIQUES

There are several techniques that can be used to troubleshoot issues in Python code (Matthes, 2023), including:

- Debugging: This involves using a debugger to step through the code and examine the values of variables and expressions. Debugging can be done using a graphical debugger or a command-line debugger like pdb.
- Error messages: Python provides detailed error messages that can be used to diagnose issues with the code. The error messages can be used to identify the line of code that is causing the problem and the type of error that has occurred.
- Print statements: This is a simple but effective technique that involves adding print statements to the code to display the values of variables and expressions. This can be used to track the flow of the code and identify any unexpected behavior.
- Unit testing: Writing unit tests can help you to identify issues with specific units of code. By testing individual units of code, you can isolate and fix problems before they affect the rest of the system.
- Google and Stack Overflow: These are online communities that provide answers to programming questions. If you encounter an issue that you can't resolve, you can often find helpful answers by searching for the error message or a similar problem on these websites.

- Code reviews: This is a process in which other developers review your code to identify any potential issues. Code reviews can be an effective way to catch bugs and improve the overall quality of your code.

These are just a few of the many techniques that can be used to troubleshoot issues in Python code. The best technique will depend on the nature of the problem, your experience level, and the resources available to you.

 # Title of Code Sample: Using the pdb library to debug a Python script
 # Objective of Code Sample: This code sample demonstrates how to use the pdb library to debug a Python script.
 # Sample Code:

```
import pdb
def divide(a, b):
    pdb.set_trace()
    return a / b
result = divide(10, 2)
print(result)
```

In this example, the pdb.set_trace function is used to start the debugger. When the script is run, the debugger will start and allow you to step through the code, examine the values of variables and expressions, and perform other debugging tasks. The p command can be used to print the value of an expression, and the n command can be used to step to the next line of code. To exit the debugger, type q at the prompt.

BEST PRACTICES FOR DESIGNING DATA STRUCTURES AND ALGORITHMS

BEST PRACTICES CHECKLIST

When designing data structures and algorithms in Python, it is important to consider the following best practices (Reitz & Schlusser, 2016):

- Choose the right data structure: Different data structures have different performance characteristics, so it is important to choose the right data structure for the task at hand. For example, if you need to store a large number of items and retrieve them quickly, a hash table or a binary search tree may be a good choice.
- Avoid brute-force algorithms: Brute-force algorithms are algorithms that try all possible combinations of inputs until they find a solution. These algorithms can be very slow and should be avoided whenever possible.

- Use appropriate algorithms: Different algorithms have different performance characteristics, so it is important to choose the right algorithm for the task at hand. For example, if you need to sort a large number of items, a quicksort or a mergesort algorithm may be a good choice.
- Optimize algorithms: Algorithms can often be optimized to improve their performance. This can be done by reducing the number of operations performed, reducing the time complexity of operations, or improving the space complexity of algorithms.
- Consider the input size: It is important to consider the size of the input when designing algorithms. Some algorithms may perform well for small inputs, but become very slow for large inputs. In these cases, alternative algorithms should be considered that are more efficient for larger inputs.
- Reuse existing code: Whenever possible, existing code and libraries should be reused to reduce the time and effort required to develop a solution. This can also help to ensure that the solution is robust and well-optimized.
- Consider parallelism: When processing large amounts of data, parallel processing can be used to improve performance. Parallel processing involves dividing a large task into smaller tasks that can be performed simultaneously. This can be achieved using techniques such as multithreading, multiprocessing, or distributed processing.
- Use caching: Caching is a technique that involves storing the results of expensive computations in memory so they can be reused later. Caching can significantly improve the performance of algorithms that perform the same computations repeatedly.

These best practices can help to ensure that the data structures and algorithms you design are efficient, scalable, and robust. By considering these best practices during the design phase, you can save time and effort in the development process and deliver a high-quality solution to your users.

AVOIDING COMMON PITFALLS IN DATA STRUCTURE AND ALGORITHM DESIGN

When designing data structures and algorithms, it is crucial to avoid common pitfalls that can hinder the effectiveness and efficiency of your solutions. One such pitfall is over-engineering, where developers create overly complex data structures and algorithms that are challenging to understand and maintain (Golomb et al., 2018). While striving for robustness is important, it is essential to strike a balance and avoid unnecessary complexity that can lead to confusion and difficulties in future maintenance.

Another pitfall to avoid is ignoring edge cases. It is crucial to consider these exceptional scenarios when designing algorithms, as they can often result in unexpected behavior. By thoroughly analyzing and accounting for edge cases, developers can ensure the reliability and accuracy of their solutions. Choosing inefficient algorithms is another pitfall that can significantly impact performance. It is crucial to select algorithms that are appropriate and efficient for the task at hand. Using inefficient algorithms can lead to slow processing times, hindering overall system performance.

Reusing code without a complete understanding is a temptation that should be avoided. Copying and pasting code from online sources without fully comprehending its inner workings can result in suboptimal code (Keuning et al., 2017). The code may not be optimized for the specific use case or may contain bugs and security vulnerabilities. It is essential to thoroughly understand and validate any code being used to ensure its reliability and security. Considering scalability is of utmost importance when designing data structures and algorithms. Neglecting to account for how they will perform as data sizes increase can result in poor performance and an inability to handle large amounts of data. Careful consideration of scalability allows for solutions that can grow and adapt to changing requirements effectively.

Thorough testing is a critical step that should not be overlooked. It is essential to test data structures and algorithms rigorously, including edge cases and performance testing. This comprehensive testing approach ensures that they function correctly and efficiently. Neglecting thorough testing can lead to the presence of bugs and performance issues that may remain undiscovered until they cause significant problems in production.

Ignoring best practices is yet another pitfall to avoid. Best practices, such as using appropriate algorithms, optimizing algorithms, and considering scalability, exist for a reason. Ignoring these guidelines can result in suboptimal performance and increased development time. It is crucial to stay updated on the latest best practices and continuously improve data structure and algorithm design skills to produce high-quality, efficient solutions.

Title of Code Sample: Optimizing a sorting algorithm using the timeit library
Objective of Code Sample: The code sample below demonstrates how to use the timeit library to optimize a sorting algorithm.
Sample Code:

```
import timeit
def bubble_sort(arr):
    n = len(arr)
    for i in range(n):
        for j in range(0, n-i-1):
            if arr[j] > arr[j+1]:
                arr[j], arr[j+1] = arr[j+1], arr[j]
    return arr
arr = [64, 34, 25, 12, 22, 11, 90]
```

```
print("Sorted array is:", bubble_sort(arr))
print("Time taken:", timeit.timeit(lambda: bubble_
sort(arr), number=1000))
```

In this example, a bubble sort algorithm is defined to sort an array of numbers. The timeit library is then used to measure the time taken to sort the array 1000 times. The timeit function takes a callable object as an argument and returns the time taken to run the callable object. The number argument is used to specify the number of times the callable object should be run. The resulting time can be used to compare the performance of different sorting algorithms and identify opportunities for optimization.

PROFILING AND OPTIMIZATION

PROFILERS AND THEIR USE IN PYTHON

A *profiler* is a tool that can be used to measure the performance of a Python script. Profilers can measure the time taken to run a script, the number of function calls, and other performance metrics. Profilers can be used to identify performance bottlenecks in Python scripts (Wagner et al., 2017). By measuring the time taken to run a script and the number of function calls, it is possible to identify areas of the code that are slowing down the script. These areas can then be optimized to improve the performance of the script.

There are several profilers available for Python, including cProfile, profile, and Pyflame. cProfile is a built-in profiler in Python and is included in the standard library. It provides detailed information about the performance of a script, including the time taken to run each function, the number of calls made to each function, and the amount of memory used.

Profile is another profiler that provides a similar set of features to cProfile. The main difference between the two profilers is that profile is a pure Python implementation, while cProfile is a C extension.

Pyflame is a newer profiler that is designed specifically for Python. It provides a detailed, high-level view of the performance of a script, and it can be used to identify performance bottlenecks in real time. Pyflame also provides information about the execution of individual lines of code, which can be useful for debugging.

Using profilers is straightforward. Simply run the profiler on the script that you want to analyze, and then inspect the output to identify any performance bottlenecks. It is important to note that profilers can be resource-intensive and may slow down the script that they are profiling. As a result, it is recommended to use profilers only during development and to remove them from the production code.

Title of Code Sample: Using the cProfile library to profile a Python script
Objective of Code Sample: This code sample shows how to use the cProfile library to profile a Python script.
Sample Code:

```
import cProfile
def fib(n):
    if n <= 0:
        return 0
    elif n == 1:
        return 1
    else:
        return fib(n-1) + fib(n-2)
cProfile.run('fib(35)')
```

In this example, a simple Fibonacci function is defined to calculate the nth Fibonacci number. The cProfile library is then used to profile the function by calling the run function with the argument 'fib(35)'. The profiler will output a report that provides information on the time taken to run the function, the number of function calls, and other performance metrics. This information can be used to identify performance bottlenecks and optimize the function.

Now that we have covered the basics behind the Python programming language, we can shift our focus to looking at some further examples within library and information science. In the following chapters, we will explore topics that are relevant to the modern librarian, including the use of Python for library management and usage data, library research data support, text analysis, enriching library and information science research, and artificial intelligence applications. We will then wrap up the book with part 3, which focuses on practical and ethical considerations for using Python.

REFERENCES

Arbuckle, D. (2010). *Python testing: Beginner's guide*. Packt Publishing.
Golomb, D., Gangadharan, D., Chen, S., Sokolsky, O., & Lee, I. (2018, May). Data freshness over-engineering: Formulation and results. In *2018 IEEE 21st International Symposium on Real-Time Distributed Computing (ISORC)* (pp. 174-83). IEEE.
Kambaraliyevich, A. D. (2022). Learn how to prevent errors while writing Python code. *Texas Journal of Multidisciplinary Studies, 6*, 37-41.
Keuning, H., Heeren, B., & Jeuring, J. (2017). Code quality issues in student programs. In *Proceedings of the ACM Conference on Innovation and Technology in Computer Science Education* (pp. 110-15). Association for Computing Machinery.

Kohn, T. (2019). The error behind the message: Finding the cause of error messages in Python. In *Proceedings of the 50th ACM Technical Symposium on Computer Science Education* (pp. 524-30). Association for Computing Machinery.

Matthes, E. (2023). *Python crash course*. No Starch Press.

Redondo, J. M., & Ortin, F. (2014). A comprehensive evaluation of common Python implementations. *IEEE Software, 32*(4), 76-84.

Reitz, K., & Schlusser, T. (2016). *The hitchhiker's guide to Python: Best practices for development*. O'Reilly Media.

Sale, D. (2014). *Testing Python: Applying unit testing, TDD, BDD, and acceptance testing*. John Wiley & Sons.

Trautsch, F., & Grabowski, J. (2017, March). Are there any unit tests? An empirical study on unit testing in open source python projects. In *2017 IEEE International Conference on Software Testing, Verification and Validation (ICST)* (pp. 207-18). IEEE.

Wagner, M., Llort, G., Mercadal, E., Giménez, J., & Labarta, J. (2017). Performance analysis of parallel python applications. *Procedia Computer Science, 108*, 2171-79.

Part II

Further Applications of Python in Information Organizations

7
Library Management and Usage Data

Libraries produce a large amount of data as part of their normal operations: the number of patron visits over time, the number and types of materials used or lent by patrons, number of wifi sessions and computer uses, etc. This data from individual libraries also gets aggregated into publications and data sets, like the National Center of Education Statistic's Integrated Postsecondary Data System (NCES IPEDS) for academic libraries, and the Institute of Museum and Library Services' Public Library Survey (IMLS PLS). This data may be used by libraries to inform services offered and administrative decision-making like personnel allocation and budgeting. However, these analyses can often be at a very surface level, providing only descriptive statistics, e.g., "In January we had 84 visits and 112 materials borrowed; in February 62 visits and 101 materials borrowed. . . ." While these descriptive statistics are helpful, there is so much more power behind this data that can be unlocked with a little Python expertise.

This chapter explores three practical ways that you can use your new Python skillset to unlock insight from data that most libraries already regularly collect. The first analytical method is a frequency analysis of library use. The second is a regression analysis, also using the library use data. The final is the use of Python for managing library budgeting and finances. The examples in this chapter, which you are encouraged to work through alongside us, all primarily utilize either the IMLS's PLS or NCES IPEDS data. This data is available open access in csv format from:

- https://imls.gov/research-evaluation/data-collection/public-libraries-survey
- https://nces.ed.gov/ipeds/use-the-data

NOTE: The IMLS PLS and NCES IPEDS data that we will use in this chapter need to be cleaned before analysis. There are many libraries that provide incomplete data, and this will skew your results unless you remove these libraries prior to performing your analysis. Data with values of 0, -1, -3, and -9 signify different types of missing or incomplete data and should be removed from the dataset or else your results will substantially differ from those presented in this chapter.

FREQUENCY ANALYSIS WITH LIBRARY OPERATIONS DATA

It is vital while managing libraries to look at some indicators about patrons' visits, materials used, the available resources, and how they interact with each other (Krikelas, 1966). Having an insufficient number of staff or librarians at a highly visited library or providing more staff to a library where they are less needed will negatively impact on your services and efficiency. Frequency is a useful tool to analyze patrons' visits, resources used, and the available resources to meet the demands.

What does frequency mean? *Frequency* provides an informational summary of a dataset that is meaningful and useful. Frequency records the number of times an event happens. Frequency can be in ratio, percentage, or a scalar value. Revealing a patron visits-to-staffing ratio will provide a better understanding of resource impact, allocation, or redistribution. It is also useful information that could justify a request of additional staff, and using this information will easily convince library board members, university administrators, or any leadership in charge of library and resources to provide or approve a better resource management plan.

So, how does one perform frequency? Of course, the first step is to have your data file prepared, as discussed in part 1 of this book. The second step is to visualize your data to understand what useful frequency one would need to understand the dataset. From there, performing frequency in Python is straightforward. Just ensure that your directory paths align with what you have named your files/save paths.

The data used for our frequency examples is from the 2020 public libraries survey data of the Institute of Museum and Library (IMLS PLS). The data sample used in this section has columns of data for all the public libraries for all the US states and territories. The columns include state, library name, number of librarians and staff at each library, open hours, resources available, physical and online circulations, total yearly visits, computer and Wi-Fi uses, etc.

Imagine that you are tasked with providing an overview of daily library patron visits and website visits for all public libraries in a state (e.g., Alaska); you would need to gather data on a number of variables in order to provide a complete picture of the situation. These variables might include the daily number of patron visits, the ratio of librarian visits to patron visits, the percentage of visitors who use the library's computers and Wi-Fi, and the number of books and online materials checked out per visit. While there may be other variables that you could include, for the purposes of this example, we will focus on these key metrics.

The Python code below provides you with an example of how to calculate daily visit frequencies to both the physical library and online library services, percentage, and ratio of resource usage. The daily frequency is calculated by dividing the total visits by total hours open. We assume that each library is open eight hours a day, and online services are offered twenty-four hours a day:

Title of Code Sample: Daily frequency of patrons' library visits and website visits for each library

Objective of Code Sample: This code sample demonstrates how to use Python code in extracting relevant data from a data file. It uses patrons' related data provided by the library to extract the vital information that will help the library make an informed decision.

Sample Code: #Import all the necessary modules and the data file containing the patron's visit and website library usage

```
Import pandas as pd
```

Store the Patron's data csv file into a variable for your code to use

```
patronsData = pd.read_csv('patronsData.csv')
```

Extract data needed for the analysis from the patronsData csv file

```
PatronsVisitsData = patronsData[['State', 'LibCode', 'HrsOpen']]
```

Create all the columns needed for the data analysis results

```
PatronsVisitsData = PatronsVisitsData.reindex(columns = PatronsVisitsData.columns.tolist() + ['DailyVisitCount', 'DailyWebVisitCount', 'LibrarianRatio', 'ComputerUseRec', 'WifiUsePerc', 'BooksVisitsRatio', 'DownloadsRate', 'OnlContUseRate'])
```

Perform the frequency count for each case and put the results in their corresponding columns

```
PatronsVisitsData['DailyVisitCount'] = patronData['Visits']*8/PatronsData['HrsOpen']
PatronsVisitsData['DailyWebVisitCount'] = patronsData['WebVisit']/365
```

Calculation of ratios and percentages for patron visits and resource usage
Library-to-Visits Ratio

```
PatronsVisitsData['LibrarianRatio'] =
PatronsVisitsData['DailyVisitCount']/
patronsData['NbLibrarians']
```

Percentage of patrons that used a computer during their visit

```
PatronsVisitsData['ComputerUsePerc'] =
100*(patronsData['CompUse']/patronsData['Visits'])
```

Percentage of patrons that used Wi-Fi during their visit

```
PatronsVisitsData['WifiUsePerc'] =
100*(patronsData['WifiUse']/patronsData['Visits'])
```

Number of books checked out per patron

```
PatronsVisitsData['BooksVisitsRatio'] =
patronsData['PhysCirc']/patronsData['Visits']
```

Number of downloads per patron

```
PatronsVisitsData['DownloadsRate'] =
patronsData['onlineDown']/patronsData['WebVisit']
```

Total number of online materials viewed per patron

```
PatronsVisitsData['OnlContUseRate'] =
patronsData['OnlineContUse']/patronsData['WebVisit']
```

Rounds the result values to two decimal places

```
PatronsVisitsData = PatronsVisitsData.round(decimals = 2)
```

Displays the patrons and resources data findings, limiting to the first seven lines

```
PatronsVisitsData[1:8].sort_values(by='HrsOpen', ascending = False)
```

Using the state of Alaska as an example, the frequency calculation result shows that some libraries have more online visits than physical location visits (e.g., AK0002). All other libraries have more patrons visiting the physical locations than using online services. Additionally, locations with more opening hours tend to have more visits, except for a few locations where daily website visits were rather higher. You could see similar patterns across states, suggesting that there might be a correlation between opening hours and the number of visits. Correlation and regression analyses could confirm or affirm these findings. You can perform similar interpretations for all states or for each state to understand daily, weekly, and monthly visit patterns for both physical and website visits.

For daily visits–librarian ratio, only three out of eleven libraries have low visits-librarian (<20), suggesting that the locations with a higher ratio might need additional librarians if we perform further analysis (e.g., regression analysis) and discover the workload pattern of librarians at those locations. For instance, some libraries have a ratio of more than 190, meaning one librarian will serve, on average, 190 visitors on a daily basis. Comparing this result with other libraries with a ratio of 19, it suggests that the formal categories of libraries might need additional librarians.

For computer and Wi-Fi daily usages, about 8 to 25 percent of visitors used library computers in the state of Alaska. Having a decent number of computers will be enough to handle patrons' computer needs. Some libraries had lower computer and Wi-Fi usage but recorded higher book checkouts. This suggests that the availability of physical books and materials might be more important in these locations than computers and Wi-Fi.

For online library services, patrons of some libraries use more digital materials available online than materials available offline. The Converse County library in Wyoming, for instance, has recorded on average 10.22 resources downloaded and or used per website visit, while only 0.52 physical book checkouts per patron visit. Unlike Converse County, the Anchorage library in Alaska recorded on average two book checkouts per visit, and less than 0.5 resources used from their website.

The above example shows you the importance of frequency in understanding your library data, and it is the starting point for further data analyses. We encourage you to play around with the Python code to come up with more variables or metrics to assess patron visits and their impact on weekly and monthly resources.

REGRESSION ANALYSIS WITH LIBRARY USE DATA

Often, it is worthwhile to know more about the data you collect about your and other libraries than just frequencies. You want to know if some change you have made in your library service has had a desirable effect, or whether a potential change that is being discussed has fared well in other libraries (Dilevko, 2007). When it comes to these types of analysis, regression analysis is extremely valuable.

What is regression analysis? *Regression analysis* allows analysts to understand effects of variables upon one another across large datasets. Ordinary least squares regression analysis (the most common/standard type) reveals relationships between one or more independent variables and a single dependent variable. Understanding the relationships among variables is valuable for decision-making and advocacy. It is much easier to convince the library board or university administrator that funding should be increased, hours of operation expanded, or greater employee autonomy offered if you have numbers to back it up.

Anecdotes or descriptive numbers are valuable to a point, but generally will not be sufficient when it comes to major administrative decisions at large libraries.

So, how does one perform a regression analysis? Of course, the first step is to have your data file prepared, as discussed in part 1 of this book. From there, the code needed to perform an ordinary least squares regression in Python is straightforward. Just ensure that your directory paths align with what you have named your files/save paths. The following code will perform the task:

Title of Code Sample: Regression analysis of library resources
Objective of Code Sample: The code sample below demonstrates how to use Python code to provide insight into the effect in relationship between different library resources.
Sample Code:

Imports the libraries necessary to perform regression analysis

```
import numpy as np
import pandas as pd
from sklearn.linear_model import LinearRegression
```

Loads data into a pandas Dataframe

```
df = pd.read_csv('Sample_IMLS_Public_Libraries_Dataset.csv')
```

Creates a linear regression model object

```
model = LinearRegression()
```

Fits the model based on the 'LibOps' and 'Visits' data

```
X = df[['LibOps']]
y = df['visits']
model.fit(x, y)
```

Prints the coefficients of the model

```
print('Model Intercept (b)', model.intercept_)
print('LibOps Coefficient (m)', model.coef_[0])
```

PUBLIC LIBRARY DATA

Imagine that your library is interested in understanding the relationship between the number of hours that the library is open and the number of library visits, reference sessions, Wi-Fi sessions, and programming attendance. The IMLS PLS has all this data available for your use. You might want to start by controlling for the library service population. You can create new variables in Excel by using a simple math function. On an open column, use the formula =Visits column/library service area column (e.g., =CV2/W2). You now have a column of data that shows the number of visits per individual in a library's service area for every public library in the United States.

You can now run a regression analysis in order to understand the relationship among these variables. Based on the 2020 PLS data, you are likely to find something similar to the following when using hrsopen as your dependent variable and visitsLSA:

For hours open and visits per capita in library service area, $r^2 = .003$, $p < .001$, with a beta of .00002. This suggests that hours open plays a very small, yet statistically significant, role in the number of visits per capita that you would expect a library to receive. For each hour extra the library is open, the number of visits increases by .00002 per capita. Indeed, this is a very small number, but it is nonetheless significant from a statistical standpoint and tells you something about patron behavior. Keep in mind that if your library service area has 100,000 people, then this translates to an increase in library visits of about two people per extra hour the library is open. So, if you increased the operating hours by five hours per week, fifty weeks a year, then it would be anticipated to increase year-end total library visits by 500.

Perhaps a slightly more dramatic relationship is that between e-book collection size and library circulation. For these variables, we find $r^2 = .049$, $p < .001$, with a beta value of 1.2, suggesting that for each e-book to which the library provides access, total circulation increases by 1.2. Add 1,000 e-books to your collection? Add 1,200 checkouts to your rolls. Providing access to large e-book databases could substantially increase circulation. Adding e-books to a library that does not have many or any to start could substantially increase circulation: e-books represent only 11.1 percent of the total collections at the Irving, Texas, Public Library, but 13.9 percent of total circulation (which, if one is curious, does equal a ratio of 1.2 to 1).

ACADEMIC LIBRARY DATA

Your university has discussed whether it should increase the purchasing budget for the library in order to expand circulation of materials. Administrators are interested in knowing if there is a discernable relationship between collection size and the annual circulation per student + faculty member. All the data needed to address this question is available through the NCES IPEDS database. The following data is needed:

- Under "Academic Libraries":
    - Number of physical books
    - Number of digital/electronic books
    - Total physical library circulations
    - Total digital/electronic circulations

- Under "Human Resources":
  - Full-time instructional staff – with faculty status, on tenure track
  - Full-time instructional staff – with faculty status, tenured
- Under "Fall Enrollment":
  - Grand total - all students total

In your csv file, you can combine the totals for physical and electronic resources; physical and electronic circulation; and tenure-track, tenured faculty, and grand total of students. This will result in three variables: collectionSize, circulations, totalServicePopulation. You can then divide both collectionSize and circulations by totalServicePopulation in order to derive two variables: collectionsPer and circulationsPer. These two variables—collections per member of the library service population and circulations per member of the library service population—will be those used to evaluate the relationship between collections and circulations.

Once these variables have been calculated, you can perform an analysis just as with the public library data. collectionsPer should be your independent variable (x) and circulationsPer the dependent variable (y). The results should be similar to $r^2 = .045$, $p < .001$, with a beta of .035. This indicates that for each increase of one physical or electronic resource per student/faculty member, circulation increases by .035 per student/faculty member. So, in a school with 10,000 students and 200 instructional faculty, increasing the size of collections by one item per person (10,200 new items) would increase circulations by 3.5 percent, or 357 (10,200*.035). If an item costs $20 on average, then an investment of $204,000 in order to raise circulation by 357 may not be the most practical approach—especially when the data shows that increasing librarian salaries by that same amount (equivalent to an average raise of about $1,500 to 3,000 per library employee at most large universities like Ohio State and Texas-Austin) would predict an increase of circulation of 13 percent per person, or 1,326 for that same school of 10,200. This analysis provides justification for allocating increased funding to human resources rather than solely increasing acquisitions budgets.

Regression analysis is a powerful tool, and this will not be the last time we discuss it in this book. In future chapters, we will discuss how regression analysis can be used to support a range of organizational data and social science research projects. Regression analysis, along with other more advanced statistical approaches like structural equation modeling, cluster analysis, and ANOVA, are key to publishing your research in top scholarly journals and ensuring that the arguments that you make to administrators have a level of infallibility that makes them harder to contradict or ignore.

LIBRARY BUDGETING AND FINANCES MANAGEMENT USING PYTHON CODE

Financial management is a crucial aspect of running a successful library (Lohela & Summers, 1982). It involves creating and sticking to a budget, securing adequate funding, and making sure that the available funds are used in a way that maximizes their impact on the library and all its stakeholders. Unfortunately, many libraries struggle with financial management and may delegate this important task to outsiders who may not fully understand the specific needs of the library. As a result, it is important for libraries to have a strong understanding of financial management in order to ensure that they have the resources they need to thrive.

Imagine that you have been tasked with preparing a library budget based on the library's current needs—the payment of employee salary, the purchase of new library resources, and the allocation of finance for library programming. After preparing the budget, you are asked to compare budgets from libraries with similar characteristics and project what the future budget might look like. What will you do, and how will you approach the task?

Financial data is a crucial resource for decision-making in a library, and as a librarian, having the skills to effectively manage library finance can make a significant impact on the library's trajectory. This includes budgeting, creating compelling financial reports, and effectively communicating the story behind the data. While many libraries use spreadsheet software programs such as Microsoft Excel to manage their financial records, the analysis and processing of these documents can be limited. In order to take full advantage of the insights that financial data can provide, it may be helpful to use additional tools such as Python code to supplement traditional methods of financial analysis.

This example demonstrates how Python can be used to analyze a library budget in order to inform decision-making for the current fiscal year and beyond. The data used in this case study was sourced from the Institute of Museum and Library Services Public Library Survey (IMLS PLS) and saved as a CSV file. The raw data was then processed and analyzed using Python code to provide insights and inform the library's financial planning.

For the use case described above, we are given a set of raw financial data to analyze. Before we begin writing any Python code, it is important to observe the data and identify any potential outliers or abnormalities. This will also give us an understanding of the nature of the data.

To perform this analysis, we will need to import a number of libraries in Python. The numpy library (import numpy as numpyLibrary) will be used for data preprocessing and cleaning. The Pandas library (import pandas as pandasLibrary) is useful for analyzing and manipulating data. The datetime library (from datetime import datetime as dateTimeLibrary) allows us to work with date-related objects such as months and years. The plotly.express and plotly.graph_objects libraries (import plotly.express as plotExpressLibrary) are used to create interactive charts in our Python code. The Jupyter_dash library (from jupyter_dash import JupyterDash) is imported to create dash apps within the Jupyter environment. Finally, the dash_core_components and dash_html_components libraries (import dash_core_components as dcc; import dash_html_components as html) provide interactive user interfaces and layout options for our Python structures.

If you encounter an error message in the output of your import statements that reads "Library does not exist" or "package not found," do not panic. This simply means that some of the libraries you are trying to import are not installed by default in Jupyter Notebook. To fix this, you can use the error message to identify which libraries are missing and then run the following code in your source code to install them:

```
pip install plotly jupyter_dash dash_html_components
```

Note that all the libraries should be listed on a single line of code with a single space separating them. This will allow you to use these libraries in your Python code.

To retrieve the file we want to use for analysis, we can use the pandasLibrary.read_csv command as shown in Figure 7.1.

OTHER POSSIBLE USES OF THESE APPROACHES FOR LIBRARY MANAGEMENT

In addition to the three examples provided here, there are many other great avenues for implementing Python to improve library operations (Virkus & Garoufallou, 2019). It could be used to determine appropriate starting salaries for employees based on public data, prior hires, and a combination of experience and market size. It could fuel acquisitions processes by identifying which materials have the most use relative to their cost at purchase. It could even be used (provided a sufficiently large dataset) to recommend resources to readers based on library call numbers via cluster analysis. The possibilities are endless and we only have space to share a short few of them here. The key to any good data analyst is their inventiveness and understanding of need and appropriateness (i.e., the context that surrounds the data and the analysis performed).

This chapter clearly demonstrates the value of statistical and machine-learning approaches using Python for unlocking value from library data. Just ten to fifteen lines of code are necessary to transform those same old descriptive analyses and bland visualizations into dynamic justifications for resource allocation and library value. Even if you do not become a Python "expert," these tools will undoubtedly advance how your organization thinks about

We need to introduce some columns for the purpose of ensuring that we carryout the right analysis on the data.

```python
dataRetrieved['starts'] = list(
    map(lambda x: x.startswith('To '), dataRetrieved['Locale']))

dataRetrieved.loc[dataRetrieved.starts == True, 'category'] = "Transfer"
dataRetrieved.drop('starts', axis=1, inplace=True)
```

```python
# Introduce a date column to the data
dataRetrieved['date'] = pandasLibrary.to_datetime(dataRetrieved['date'])
# Introduce a year_month column to the data
dataRetrieved['year_month'] = dataRetrieved['date'].dt.strftime('%Y-%m')
```

Display the networth of the library over time on a chart

```python
NetWorthTable = dataRetrieved.groupby(['year_month'])['amount'].sum().reset_index(name ='sum')
NetWorthTable['cumulative sum'] = Net_Worth_Table['sum'].cumsum()
Net_Worth_Chart = go.Figure(
    data = go.Scatter(x = Net_Worth_Table["year_month"], y = Net_Worth_Table["cumulative sum"]),
    layout = go.Layout(
        title = go.layout.Title(text = "Net Worth Over Time")
    )
)
NetWorthChart.update_layout(
    xaxis_title = "Date",
    yaxis_title = "Net Worth (£)",
    hovermode = 'x unified'
)
NetWorthChart.update_xaxes(
    tickangle = 45)
NetWorthChart.show()
```

Finally, let's show the total monthly expenses on a chart

```python
dataRetrieved = dataRetrieved[dataRetrieved.category != "Capital"]
dataRetrieved.amount = df.amount*(-1)
TotalMonthlyExpensesChart = df.groupby
(['year_month'])['amount'].sum().reset_index(name = 'sum')
TotalMonthlyExpensesChart = px.bar
(Total_Monthly_Expenses_Table, x = "year_month", y = "sum", title = "Total Monthly Expenses")
TotalMonthlyExpensesChart.update_yaxes
(title = 'Expenses ($)', visible = True, showticklabels = True)
TotalMonthlyExpensesChart.update_xaxes
(title = 'Date', visible = True, showticklabels = True)
TotalMonthlyExpensesChart.show()
```

Figure 7.1. Calculating a Library's Net Value
Source: The authors

the value of its own data, what it can reveal about human behavior, and why it is absolutely imperative to ensure that organizations like libraries that store considerable amounts of data do so in a secure manner.

In subsequent chapters, we will discuss other valuable uses of Python in the areas of research data services, text analysis (for research and library management purposes), for your own personal library and information science research, and for some more advanced artificial intelligence (AI) applications that will advance your organizational mission. At any time, if you get lost with terminology or concepts, be sure to refer back to part 1 of this book or the index in order to get back on track. Our aim is to make the process of implementing Python in your organization's operations as straightforward and pleasurable as possible!

REFERENCES

Dilevko, J. (2007). Inferential statistics and librarianship. *Library and Information Science Research, 29*(2), 209-29.

Lohela, S., & Summers, F. W. (1982). The impact of planning on budgeting. *Journal of Library Administration, 2*(2), 173-85.

Krikelas, J. (1966). Library statistics and the measurement of library services. *ALA Bulletin, 60*(5), 494-99.

Virkus, S., & Garoufallou, E. (2019). Data science from a library and information science perspective. *Data Technologies and Applications, 53*(4), 422-41.

8

Library Research Data Management

One of the main purposes of the academic library is to serve the research needs of the university. While Python is useful for a variety of library functions, research data support may be the most commonly encountered use of this language. As such, it is only natural that we dedicate a chapter of this book to how Python and related technologies can be used to support researchers. We will begin the chapter discussing the importance of an institutional data repository for supporting the storage and use of data and ensuring that it is presented in a format that is readily compatible with Python. We will then discuss how to use Python to help manage and store data and export data for usage. We will conclude by discussing a few additional considerations for research data management and the Python language.

CHOOSING AND SETTING UP AN INSTITUTIONAL REPOSITORY

Institutional repositories are important for storing knowledge and datasets produced by the researchers at a college or university. While ownership of intellectual property in the form of peer-reviewed and copyedited versions of manuscripts may be transferred to publishers, the original research products remain the right of the higher education institutions to share. The ease with which those institutional products can be accessed can have a tremendous impact on their usage. Many academic libraries already have some kind of institutional repository. If that is the case for you and your library (and you are happy with what you have), then congratulations! You can move on to the next section of this chapter. For those who do not have an institutional repository or want to try something new, read on!

What is needed for an institutional data repository? The answer to this question depends on your interests and those of your university administrators.

Do you want to opt for a commercial product? If so, they will likely make everything quite easy for you and you need not read further either. But, of course, commercial products come with commercial costs, and those are often prohibitive for smaller colleges and universities. Also, keep in mind that a fair number of these commercial platforms are designed with traditional information resources in mind. Certain metadata and formatting options that work best for analysis with Python may not be well-supported by traditional institutional repository platforms (Pittard & Li, 2020).

One other solution that requires minimal technical effort is to opt for participation in Harvard University's Dataverse project (https://dataverse.harvard.edu). The Dataverse is a huge repository hosted by Harvard, which aggregates research datasets from around the world. Individual researchers can create an account using their institutional affiliation and then directly upload documents to the repository. Of course, the drawback of this platform is that stewardship of the data falls to Harvard University, not the researcher's university. The repository is also self-curated, meaning that that there is little oversight and limited support available—the extent to which different features and quality metadata are applied varies tremendously (Boyd, 2021). For this reason, a low-cost, university-specific data repository is likely to be preferred by most higher education institutions.

If you want to go the low-cost, high-control path, DSpace is the obvious choice. It has been used by hundreds of universities for over two decades. DSpace can be installed from dspace.lyrasis.org. It must be installed in two stages: first, the back-end content; then the front-end content, or user interface. DSpace repositories can be integrated alongside the existing library web platform via hyperlinking and are customizable according to a library's needs. Though fairly simplistic in terms of layout, DSpace is intuitive for creators and users alike, with creators being able to upload metadata and other content in batches using csv files, and users able to navigate the content using search box and/or faceted searching, much like with traditional online library catalogs. It may not be the fanciest platform, but it is tried and true and can handle a variety of data formats. Dryad (https://datadryad.org/stash) is an example of a large public data repository that has been built within the DSpace environment (White et al., 2008).

A slightly less conventional option is for a school to create a GitHub channel or have a page that links out to individual researchers' channels. The benefit of GitHub is that it is most certainly designed to support the sharing of data. It is a platform with which most researchers who work with large sets of quantitative data will be familiar and already have an account. Two major drawbacks of this platform, however, are that it may not be as user friendly to qualitative or infrequent quantitative researchers that do not regularly use GitHub and, as with the Harvard Dataverse, a data repository on GitHub would require giving certain permissions and storage over to a third party.

Regardless of which repository option is selected, the most important thing to ensure is a good user experience. If researchers do not like using your platform, then they will seek alternatives like personal GitHub pages. As a library, the aim needs to be to support researchers with the tools they value, which is why acquiring data management and Python skills is valuable now and will only become more so in years to come.

PROCESSING RESEARCH DATA IN DIFFERENT FORMATS

Public, academic, special, and even school libraries are often faced with the challenge of managing research materials. Patrons who make use of research-related materials often place special requests on them. For example, a patron may request that a library provide a single digital file of different volumes from a journal. Such request may require the librarian to combine different files of the requested volumes into one single whole file. Again, for research purposes, a patron may request that some articles with specific criteria—title, subject, author name, edition, volume, etc.—from a journal be made available in different formats, while extracting their metadata.

For the two instances mentioned above, the librarian would have to do a little more work, other than his searching and retrieval skills, to get around meeting the request of the patrons. And to do this in a traditional way is no simple task. In some cases, it might take a day, if not two, for a librarian to provide a patron with such a special request—considering he has other patrons to attend to. But thank goodness, with the help of Python code, librarians stand the chance to meet the research needs of their patrons, especially when those needs fall under the special request category.

In this Python use case, we will assume that a patron placed one of those special requests. But unlike the ones mentioned above, this request is even more challenging. The patron is requesting that you provide metadata of five articles from a single journal. All the metadata—author's name, title of article, subject etc.—should be placed in an MS Excel file where the patron tends to use it for research purposes.

As you have learned from previous chapters, before starting to code, it's crucial to understand the problem and devise a logical approach to solve it. In the case of the special request from the patron, we can deduce that we need to write code that gathers metadata from acquired journal articles. Subsequently, we will need additional code to save this extracted metadata in an MS Excel file, as requested by the patron.

The code snippet below presents a solution to this problem:

Title of Code Sample: How to process research data in different formats
Objective of Code Sample: The code sample below demonstrates how to process research data that is stored in different formats.

Sample Code:

Import necessary libraries

```
import PyPDF2
import pandas as pd
```

Open pdf file and extract metadata

```
with open('example_journal.pdf', 'rb') as file:
    pdf_reader = PyPDF2.PdfFileReader(file)
    pdf_info = pdf_reader.getDocumentInfo()
```

Print extracted metadata

```
print(pdf_info)
```

Save extracted metadata to Excel file

```
data = {'Author': pdf_info.author, 'Title': pdf_info.title, 'Subject': pdf_info.subject}
df = pd.DataFrame(data, index=[0])
df.to_excel('metadata.xlsx')
```

As always, we must first install all dependency (required) libraries and have them imported into our code. The first two lines explained how to do so. Then the subsequent line of code with their comments demonstrate how to extract the metadata from the journal article pdf file. In this example, we made sure to place the pdf file in the same directory/folder as our source code. Then we type in the name of the file as a string literal on line 55.

The output can be seen at the end showing the metadata information of the file. This metadata are gotten from the file itself not the content of the file. Hence, it does describe the article in such a way as to inform one about the file and not the contents of the file. To make this interesting, we can use previous coding knowledge from this book to export the output we got from the code into an MS Excel file (please refer to chapter 5 on how to export an output into an Excel file).

Now that you have your result, one last thing to do is to have it handy so you can share it with the patron who placed the request. It is important to go through the result and manually check for inconsistencies or any form of error in the representation of the metadata before sending the file to the patron. Also, one must let the patron know about any copyright or privacy measures that should be put into consideration while using the extracted metadata.

USING PYTHON TO HELP STORE RESEARCH DATA

Storing research data is critical in any industry that relies on research activities or data to operate; an information professional might need to store various research data for future use. Data storage consists of retaining data through recording media using computing resources.

It is easier to lose your research dataset or other researchers' data because the data storage step is missing or it is incorrectly done. One of the authors of this book had a similar experience regarding the importance of data storage and its potential consequences. In my case, I was involved in a deep learning research project alongside a team of data science and machine learning professionals. One of my responsibilities was to preprocess a large image dataset, which took approximately forty-eight hours to complete. After the preprocessing was done, I stored the preprocessed data in a secure location before sharing it with the team. However, just two days before our project's completion, we encountered a major setback—we lost the preprocessed dataset that was crucial for our work. Fortunately, due to my prior caution, it only took me a few minutes to run a Python code and retrieve another copy of the dataset from my storage. This incident served as a valuable lesson, highlighting the importance of properly storing and safeguarding research datasets, whether they are our own or those of other researchers.

When an information professional or researcher wants to store research data, there are various questions they need to address before starting research data storage; a few of these questions are:

1. What is the data type I am storing? The data type could help you decide on the correct storage format; it is a good idea to store tabular data in an appropriate storage format for easy retrieval and usability; it might be inconvenient have an image file stored in text format.
2. What is the data structure? data structure is helpful for efficient data persistence and storage forms identification; a file storage has a different purpose from block storage or object storage. Storing integer data and storing string or text-based data in the same format might lead to unusable data.
3. What is the purpose of the data that needs to be stored? There are different types of research data in terms of data processing or transformation stages; storing raw and unprocessed dataset for future processing might dictate storage approach, format, location, and tools to ensure easy retrieval and processing of the data; and a data processing engine could also indicate the data storage format required as input. Microsoft Office Excel cannot open a pdf file without a file conversion, and it is better to save tabular data in Excel-compatible data format.
4. What are the legal and ethical requirements for the data? You cannot store research data that involve human subjects as you would with other data; some data storage requires encryption and must be done during the storage of the data.

This list is not exhaustive, and anyone could add more questions to the list to fit their personal needs. We all know that Python is a programming and scripting language, not a storage media or tool; Python assists during data storage; for example, Python provides some libraries such as sqlite3 pickles to store objects' data. Other Python libraries could assist in storing and manipulating a large amount of data like Pillow, lmdb, and h5py. The previous questions listed are critical to determining the most appropriate method to store research data or any research-related dataset. You can store data on disk in various formats; or using lightning memory-mapped databases (LMDB); or hierarchical data format (HDF5); several other methods of storing research data exist.

Storing research data could follow the following steps:

Step 1: Define your data storage function and or data retrieval function: At this step, you define a Python function to store your data based on the storage approach you want to use. The advantage of defining a storage function is its reusability for storing multiple and different datasets. It is optional to define a retrieval function; however, it is a best practice to define this function to test the data stored to avoid data loss. A research best practice to recommend is to add exception handling and logging to your data storage function.

Step 2: Research data manipulation, processing, and preparation for storage: This stage deals with the research data in the desired processing stage (raw data, research analysis results, processed data, etc.) and format (flat files, images, etc.). At this stage, you prepare for data storage by defining all the storage parameters, storage locations (local disk, remote, databases, cloud), and any connection to the storage location. You can also define the data file name for storage with the Python programming language.

Step 3: Data storage processing: This stage consists of calling your storage function (defined in step 1) and providing this function with all the parameters to store your data in the assigned location.

Step 4: Verify a successful storage processing: Verification is crucial for data storage, especially when you are working with in-memory data. Successful data storage requires a good verification of the data stored in the desired format and at the location specified. You can use any method to check that your data is correctly stored. I recommend the use of a data retrieval function (defined in step 1) to pull the data stored or its portion to verify the data you stored in step 3.

Our use case will cover the storage of research analysis results data. Assume you perform a lab test on a group of adults to assess whether they pass the test or not. You want to know if there is any correlation between some of their physiological variables (such as glucose level, blood pressure, BMI, and age). In our case, we want to focus on people that pass the lab test. After the test, you collect your data and analyze it with Python; however, if you close your program, you will lose all your non-persistent data. You want to store the results and use them in your report or for further analysis.

The test data used for this case was a random lab dataset generated in CSV format. The dataset has six columns (individual id, glucose level, blood pressure, BMI, age, and whether the individual passes or fails the test) and 267 rows. The code snippet below provides a Python code sample of storing your analyzed data in column format.

Title of Code Sample: How to store research data
Objective of Code Sample: The code sample below shows how you can go about storing research analysis data for your library or information organization.
Sample Code:

```python
#Import libraries

import pandas as pd
import pickle

#Import the lab test data and check the first row

LabData = pd.read_csv('Labtest.csv')
LabData.head()

# Define a function that will store your research data analysis

def store_Data(Data, OutputName):
    try:
      with open(OutputName, "wb") as fw:
         pickle.dump(Data, fw)
    except Exception as ex:
         print("Error during storing the data", ex)
    fw.close()

# Define a function that can call or retrieve your stored data

def retrieve_Data(filename):
    try:
      with open(filename, "rb") as fw:
         return pickle.load(fw)
    except Exception as ex:
         print("Error during retrieving the stored
         data:", ex)

#Perform a correlation analysis on dataset of people who passed the test

Data = LabData.loc[(LabData['Pass test?'] == 1)].drop(['Pass test?', 'Individual ID'], axis = 1)
```

```
Results = Data.corr()
OutputFile = 'CorrelationTestResults'
store_Data(Results, OutputFile)
```

#Call your stored data

```
RetrievedData = retrieve_Data("CorrelationTestResults")
print(RetrievedData)
```

In our case, we use pickle library to store our analysis results data. We import the raw data and check the first two rows of the data. We then define the storage function called "store_Data" and the retrieval function called "retrieve_Data." Both functions have errors or exception handling. The storage function gets two input parameters and process the storage of the dataset provided as input to the function. The first parameter is the data to be stored, and the second is the output name we provide to the analysis result data. After defining these two functions, we perform our correlation analysis and assign the result to a variable called "Results." We then provide this variable to our storage function for processing. Our result is stored as a flat file and named "CorrelationTestResults" by calling our storage function. We check the correlation analysis results data stored by calling the retrieve data function.

A FEW ADDITIONAL CONSIDERATIONS FOR PYTHON AND RDM

A talented research data analyst may be able to perform analyses as a member of a research team, rather than serve a role largely as a steward of data. It is the hope that the chapters in part 1 of this book, as well as those in the prior and future chapters in this section, will enable the reader to fulfill that type of role. Indeed, many of the most popular statistical analyses for quantitative researchers (aside from "hard-core data scientists") include correlation analysis, regression analysis, and cluster analysis, which have all been discussed already in earlier sections of this book (Bruce et al., 2020).

Of course, when working with researchers, it is necessary to be flexible to the needs of a given project and be responsive to rather quick-paced changes. As illustrated in the introduction of this book, it has only been in the past few years that Python really emerged as the most prominent language for data science and statistical analysis. While it is unlikely that Python's popularity will suddenly drop, given its user friendliness, it is possible that the ways in which it is used by researchers could change. Certain syntax or popular packages may change over time and with new versions of Python, which may require adjustments to repositories, and will certainly require continuous learning for the data analyst or data librarian to remain relevant and provide the best service to their patrons and collaborators.

REFERENCES

Boyd, C. (2021). Use of optional data curation features by users of Harvard Dataverse Repository. *Journal of eScience Librarianship, 10*(2), article 1. https://doi.org/10.7191/jeslib.2021.1191.

Bruce, P., Bruce, A., Gedeck, P. (2020). *Practical statistics for data scientists.* Sebastopol, CA: O'Reilly Media, Inc.

Pittard, W. S., & Li, S. (2020). The essential toolbox of data science: Python, R, Git, and Docker. In Li, S. (ed.), *Computational Methods and Data Analysis for Metabolomics.* New York, NY: Humana.

White, H., Carrier, S., Thompson, A., Greenberg, J., & Scherle, R. (2008). The Dryad data repository: A Singapore framework metadata architecture in a DSpace environment. In *Proceedings of the International Conference on Dublin Core and Metadata Applications, 2008,* 157–62.

9
Text Analysis

Text analysis is a computational method employed to extract meaning from a series of texts (Underwood, 2015). While librarians are no strangers to this technique, particularly in the context of finding connections or significance across various texts, it often necessitates the use of different toolsets to cater to patrons' information needs. Thus, this chapter aims to explore the diverse use cases of Python in text analysis, elucidate the importance of utilizing Python in such scenarios, provide guidance on implementing Python codes to address pertinent real-life situations, and shed light on crucial considerations during code implementation.

Library services, particularly those involving research, frequently incorporate innovative tools, such as software or computer programs, for analyzing texts and unraveling their interconnections. However, utilizing such tools typically requires specialized training to comprehend their functionalities. Furthermore, proprietary software often restricts customization or addition of new features. Consequently, employing Python programming offers a significant advantage in text analysis by enabling customization of features tailored to specific analysis requirements. Python code can be easily modified or expanded to accommodate new requests from patrons.

Patrons may seek Python solutions for a range of text analysis use cases, guided by their information needs and areas of interest (Qian & Gui, 2021). Often, their requirements in text analysis revolve around quantitative research. For example, they might request assistance in determining the frequency of specific words or phrases within a given context. This quantitative approach provides insights into the significance or variation of words as they appear across different contexts or volumes.

When librarians engage in text analysis using software or programming languages like Python, they often face the challenge of acquainting themselves with the necessary steps for a successful analysis. The specific steps may vary depending on the complexity of the research request and information needs.

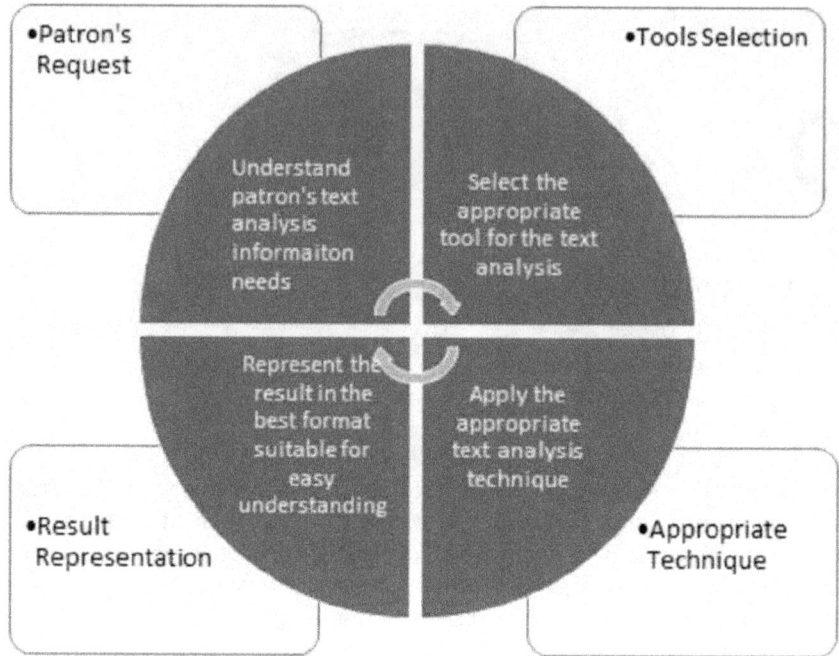

Figure 9.1. Text Analysis Model: Steps for Conducting Text Analysis
Source: The authors

However, there are overarching patterns that persist across cases (Rockwell, 2003). Therefore, the following model outlines a high-level overview of the steps involved in conducting text analysis.

The model presented in Figure 9.1 outlines four general steps involved in text analysis. Let's provide a detailed explanation of each step as described in the model:

1. Understanding the Patron's Request: Before initiating any research, librarians must grasp the information needs of the patron regarding text analysis. This step is critical to delivering a solution that aligns with the clientele's requirements. Asking appropriate questions is essential when there is ambiguity or lack of clarity. These questions help elucidate the type of text analysis the patron desires, enabling the identification of the most suitable tools. Additionally, questions about the desired format for presenting the results aid in tailoring the outcome to the patron's preferences.

2. Selection of Tools: Numerous options exist for text analysis tools. However, the patron's request should guide librarians in choosing the appropriate tool for the analysis. For example, if the patron simply requests word frequency counts in a specific book or chapter, using a complex tool would be unnecessary. It can be challenging for librarians without experience or

knowledge of the available toolsets to determine the most suitable option. The realm of text analysis tools is constantly expanding, with examples including DiscoverText, Google Cloud Natural Language API, Lexalytics Salience, and IBM SPSS Text Analytics. However, with Python code, it is not necessary to possess knowledge of a wide range of toolsets, as one can write code specifically tailored to the patron's text analysis request.

3. Selection of Appropriate Technique: A comprehensive understanding of the text analysis technique to employ is crucial. Identifying the appropriate technique informs the development of the necessary Python code or the decision to utilize an alternative analysis tool. Based on the patron's request, it becomes evident whether quantitative research, such as word count analysis, or qualitative research, such as analyzing word relationships or conducting sentiment analysis, is required.

4. Result Representation: Not all information derived from data analysis or provided to patrons can be easily understood. The confusion or inability to derive the intended benefit often arises from using improper representation methods. The format or means of presenting information is as important as the information itself. Consequently, Python code should yield results that patrons can easily comprehend. Examples of suitable formats for representing text analysis results using Python include graphical representation, visualization, modeling, and diagrams.

It is crucial to reiterate that understanding the patron's text analysis needs is paramount before implementing the aforementioned steps. The clearer the requirements for text analysis using Python code, the more effectively librarians can utilize the sample codes shared in this chapter. While Python code is highly recommended for solving the text analysis challenges mentioned, it's worth noting that there are alternative tools available, some of which were mentioned earlier, that can also address text analysis tasks.

WORD FREQUENCY ANALYSIS

In many scenarios, it is valuable to determine the frequency of words in a text or book. Word frequency refers to the number of times a specific word is used or mentioned in a text. Knowing the frequency of certain words has numerous applications, such as identifying word frequency effects, qualitative research data analysis, literature surveys, sentiment analysis, and consumer behavior analysis. In the realm of information and library science, word frequency analysis is useful for cataloging and understanding patrons' material preferences. For example, a library may want to identify the most commonly used words by online patrons when searching for books or other materials. This information enables the library to allocate appropriate resources and adjust their collection accordingly.

What is word frequency analysis? *Word frequency analysis* is a technique that allows individuals to assess the significance of different words in a text by tallying the number of occurrences of each word. This analysis can be based on absolute counts, relative frequency, or percentages. It facilitates the extraction of useful information, summarization of content, and identification of main ideas from various sources, such as student or patron feedback, research interview transcripts, emails, written documents, and websites. Word frequency analysis, in conjunction with text mining, finds applications in almost every field and industry, extending beyond information professionals.

So, how does one perform word frequency analysis?

To conduct a word frequency analysis, you need a document, text, or report in a compatible format that can be processed using word frequency analysis tools. Various tools, websites, and software applications are available for this purpose. In this book, we utilize the Python programming language due to its flexibility and simplicity for performing such analyses on any text document. You can follow the suggested steps for your word frequency analysis:

1. Select your word frequency analysis tool (e.g., Python).
2. Gather your document or text in the appropriate format and ensure it is accessible to the chosen tool.
3. Prepare the document or text by performing necessary cleanup tasks, such as tokenization and stemming, as discussed in the previous section.
4. Perform the word frequency analysis using the selected tool. In the case of Python, libraries like "wordfreq" or "counter" can be employed for this purpose.

Let's consider a practical scenario in which a library aims to understand the online behavior of its patrons in terms of the types of materials they read or access on the website. The library's IT department provides a log file that contains records of each visitor's searched, accessed, or read materials. The file has already been cleaned and prepared for analysis.

This data is oversimplified for clarity and simplicity. However, the concept will be the same whether you have a large or a messier dataset. Accurate word frequency count mostly depends on the quality of the data preparation. It is vital to ensure that you clean correctly and prepare your data to have results that will serve for important decision-making.

Figure 9.2 provides a code sample of word frequency analysis and shows the outcome of the analysis.

The results show that most online library patrons search, access, or read materials related to history subjects. These results could help to know the patrons' behavior regarding subjects they search or access most often through the website. Similarly, patrons also more often search and read materials related to mathematics. History and humanity materials are used less through the library online service. Library leadership can use this information to provide adequate resources and support to enable outstanding customer service. There are many use cases where word frequency analysis provides useful information or insight

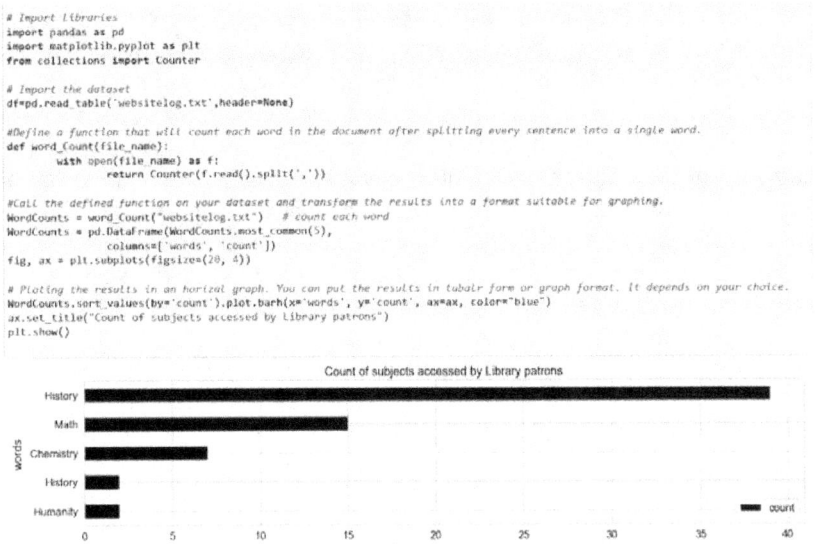

Figure 9.2. Word Frequency Analysis Code and Outcome
Source: The authors

for information professionals. This example is to teach you the basics about word frequency analysis; you could find other examples with more advanced word frequency analysis.

SENTIMENT ANALYSIS

Sentiment analysis has become essential for text classification in customer experience-related data. Many companies rely on sentiment analysis to gain insights into their customers' preferences, improve existing product quality, and make informed decisions. It serves as a valuable tool for organizations, providing leaders with insights into specific groups of people, from employees to clients. With the availability of social media data, the emergence of big data, advanced machine learning tools, and artificial intelligence, sentiment analysis has reached its peak performance (Hussein, 2018). In the context of information professionals, sentiment analysis proves useful for detecting areas of dissatisfaction in information and digital services. It is a critical research area for information researchers, enabling them to uncover untapped knowledge about people and cultures. Librarians can rely on sentiment analysis to enhance their services for patrons.

What is sentiment analysis? It is a subset of text classification within Natural Language Processing (NLP) (Medhat et al., 2014). *Sentiment analysis* involves grouping or classifying text or words into different sentiment categories such as positive, negative, good, bad, neutral, etc. However, caution must be exercised when conducting sentiment analysis in a broader context, as improper analysis can be misleading. Sentiment analysis holds significance for information professionals in various scenarios. For example, companies may be interested in assessing their performance regarding information access, sharing, and use. As an information professional, you can employ sentiment analysis to provide genuine insights on this topic to your colleagues and leadership. Libraries can also utilize this tool to improve their services and cater to the needs of their customers. Additionally, data scientists play a crucial role in developing, utilizing, and sharing sentiment analysis tools and techniques.

How can you perform sentiment analysis using Python? There are several methods to conduct sentiment analysis using Python, each with its own advantages and disadvantages. The choice may also depend on personal preferences. Some popular approaches include using libraries like TextBlob, VADER, Bag of Words Vectorization-based models, LSTM-based models, or transformer-based models, among others. Python employs a well-trained library, known as a dictionary or lexicon, for sentiment analysis. This library can be pre-trained and readily available, such as Valence Aware Dictionary and Sentiment Reasoner (VADER). Alternatively, you can create your own dictionary and train your sentiment analysis model. The sentiment analysis dictionary consists of a list of words or phrases labeled as positive, neutral, or negative based on the semantic orientation of the word. For example, a dictionary may label the word *happy* as "positive" and the word *lost* as "negative." The labeling of words may vary between dictionaries, and you can create your own if none suit your requirements. It's important to note that certain dictionaries are more suitable for sentiment analysis of comments and reviews from common applications like social media posts, while others may be tailored for specific situations.

Due to the breadth of sentiment analysis techniques, it is not possible to cover all aspects in this book. For our specific use case, we will use:

VADER: This module is part of the Natural Language Toolkit (NLTK) libraries. Utilizing VADER provides additional information in the form of a polarity score. The polarity score indicates the intensity of negativity or positivity associated with a word. The score ranges from -1 to +1, where -1 to -0.5 represents negative sentiment, -0.5 to 0.5 indicates neutral sentiment, and +0.5 to +1 signifies positive sentiment.

We will use a library survey dataset for our analysis. The dataset comprises responses from a survey conducted by a library to assess patrons' perceptions of the offered services. The library provides both online and physical location services, which are identical in nature. The dataset, available in xlsx format, is relatively small, containing three columns (service type, patron's survey ID, and their review of the services) and fifty rows (fifty participants).

The library's leadership seeks to understand how patrons perceive their services and if any differences exist between the online and physical locations. To address these questions, they conducted a survey with fifty participants and provided you with the data for sentiment analysis.

Figure 9.3 provides a code snippet and shows the outcome of a sentiment analysis.

```python
nltk.download('vader_lexicon')

#Import the raw data for sentiment analysis
rawData = pd.read_excel(r'librarySurveyData.xlsx')

# Adding an id row to the data frame, this column will serve as a lookup column to merge the result table and the raw data table
rawData["row_id"] = rawData.index + 1

#Create a new data frame with "row id" and "response" fields
sentimentData = rawData[['row_id', 'Response']].copy()

#Remove all non-aphabet characters and convert to lower case
sentimentData['Response'] = sentimentData['Response'].str.replace("[^a-zA-Z#]", " ")
sentimentData['Response'] = sentimentData['Response'].str.casefold()

#Create a new data frame to input the sentiment analysis result for each patron and display the results
sentimentAnalyseResults=pd.DataFrame()
sentimentAnalyseResults['row_id']=['99999999999']  #Initialize the data frame column row-id
sentimentAnalyseResults['sentiment_type']='NA'    #Initialize the data frame column sentiment type
sentimentAnalyseResults['sentiment_score']=0      #Initialize the data frame column sentiment score
sentimentAnalyzer = SentimentIntensityAnalyzer()
results = sentimentAnalyseResults
for index, row in sentimentData.iterrows():
    scores = sentimentAnalyzer.polarity_scores(row[1])
    for key, value in scores.items():
        temp = [key,value,row[0]]
        sentimentAnalyseResults['row_id']=row[0]
        sentimentAnalyseResults['sentiment_type']=key
        sentimentAnalyseResults['sentiment_score']=value
        results=results.append(sentimentAnalyseResults)
#Only focus on the compound polarity score for this analysis and display
resultsCleaned = results[results.sentiment_type == 'compound']
resultsCleaned.head(1)
```

	row_id	sentiment_type	sentiment_score
0	1	compound	0.8147

```python
#Visualize the sentiment analysis result by provideing some statistics and graphs
# Merge the raw data and the result data frames
resultsFinal = pd.merge(rawData, resultsCleaned, on='row_id', how='inner')

#Visualize the results using seaborn library
sns.boxplot(x='Service_type', y='sentiment_score', notch = True,
            data=resultsFinal, showfliers=False).set(title='Sentiment Score by Service type')
plt.xlabel('Service type')
plt.ylabel('Sentiment Score')
plt.xticks(rotation=0)
print("Summry Statistics of the analysis")
print(resultsCleaned ['sentiment_score'].describe())  # provide the summary statitsitcs for the sentiment analysis
```

```
Summry Statistics of the analysis
count    50.000000
mean      0.083122
std       0.521960
min      -0.669600
25%      -0.458800
50%       0.000000
75%       0.493900
max       0.876400
Name: sentiment_score, dtype: float64
```

Figure 9.3. Sentiment Analysis Code and Results
Source: The authors

The code snippet above shows you how to perform the analysis. The below code snippet shows you how to visualize and present your results to answer the two questions the leadership wants to know.

From the results, it is evident that patrons had a neutral sentiment regarding the services offered by the library. The average score falls within the range of -0.5 to 0.5, indicating a neutral sentiment. The sentiment scores range from -0.67 to 0.88, with a standard deviation of 0.5. It is important to note that patrons' feelings about the library services vary significantly from person to person. However, a large portion, up to 75 percent of the participants, expressed more neutral feelings about the services. This information can be valuable for the library's leadership and management to conduct further investigation and analysis in order to identify any areas of concern.

Now, let us compare the two service types: online services and physical location services. Both fall within the neutral range, with scores of -0.25 and -0.08, respectively. However, participants expressed more negative feelings towards physical location services compared to online services. To gain additional insights that cannot be obtained from average scores alone, we can utilize the Seaborn library and boxplot tool.

Looking at the image above, the box for both library and online services shows a wider spread in the sentiment scores of the participants' responses. This spread indicates a polarization within each service type, suggesting that some participants feel strongly positive about the services offered, while others feel strongly negative.

This insight can provide some direction regarding the specific service(s) that people with negative sentiment are receiving. It is possible that participants are expressing dissatisfaction with the limited availability of materials related to a specific subject. Therefore, the service type may be irrelevant to their overall perceptions. You can convey to the library leadership that, in general, participants have similar sentiments regardless of the service type, although there is a slightly more negative sentiment towards physical library services compared to online services. Further analysis will be necessary to pinpoint the specific services that are receiving negative feedback in order to understand the source of their dissatisfaction.

This chapter has delved into the realm of text analysis and explored the diverse use cases of Python in this field. By utilizing Python programming, librarians have the flexibility to customize and adapt their text analysis approaches to cater to the specific needs of their patrons. Emphasizing the importance of understanding patrons' requests, selecting suitable tools and techniques, and presenting results in a clear manner, the chapter provides a comprehensive framework for librarians to follow when conducting text analysis. Moreover, the chapter delves into two specific applications of text analysis: word frequency analysis and sentiment analysis. Word frequency analysis helps librarians identify patterns and preferences among patrons, while sentiment analysis assists in evaluating perceptions and pinpointing areas for service improvement. Python and various libraries like VADER empower librarians to efficiently analyze text data and extract valuable insights.

REFERENCES

Hussein, D. M. (2018). A survey on sentiment analysis challenges. *Journal of King Saud University—Engineering Sciences, 30*(4), 330-38.

Medhat, W., Hassan, A., & Korashy, H. (2014). Sentiment analysis algorithms and applications: A survey. *Ains Shams Engineering Journal, 5*(4), 1093-113.

Qian, Y., & Gui, W. (2021). Identifying health information needs of senior online communities users: A text mining approach. *Aslib Journal of Information Management, 73*(1), 5-24.

Rockwell, G. (2003). What is text analysis, really? *Literary and Linguistic Computing, 18*(2), 209-19.

Underwood, T. (2015). Seven Ways Humanists are Using Computers to Understand Text. The Stone and the Shell. Accessed April 19, 2017. https://tedunderwood.com/2015/06/04/seven-ways-humanists-are-using-computers-to-understand-text/.

10

Library and Information Science Research

In this chapter, we will delve into the applications of Python in library and information science (LIS) research, emphasizing its significance for LIS professionals, particularly in academic libraries. As stewards of knowledge and information, it is essential for LIS professionals to contribute to the advancement of their discipline and professions. Therefore, we will explore three specific applications of Python that can greatly enhance research in LIS: data analysis and visualization, text analysis and natural language processing (NLP), and web scraping and data extraction. These tools empower researchers to analyze complex datasets, process and analyze text and qualitative data, and extract relevant information from the web for research purposes. Throughout this chapter, we will provide practical examples that utilize popular libraries like Pandas, NumPy, and Beautiful Soup, equipping you with the necessary skills to incorporate these tools into your future research endeavors.

First, let us acknowledge the intrinsic value of research within the librarianship profession. Research plays a vital role in enabling librarians to stay informed about the latest developments in the field, explore emerging technologies and tools, and devise innovative solutions to challenges faced by libraries (Rubin, 2017). Moreover, research enables librarians to gain a deeper understanding of the needs and preferences of their patrons, design effective library services and programs, and evaluate the impact of their initiatives.

Conducting research also offers librarians the opportunity to contribute to the larger body of knowledge in the field and disseminate their findings to colleagues and the wider community (Lund & Wang, 2021). This not only advances the profession as a whole but also enhances the reputation of individual librarians and their institutions. Furthermore, research skills are essential for librarians, as they often collaborate with researchers and students who rely on their expertise in finding and evaluating information. Proficiency in research empowers librarians to better support these patrons, guiding them in conducting their own research effectively.

While various research methods exist, case studies have gained popularity in library and information science (Lund & Wang, 2021). However, the findings from a single case study may not possess high levels of generalizability, as the circumstances and outcomes of one library may not necessarily apply to another. On the other hand, data-based studies employing qualitative or quantitative data tend to exhibit greater rigor. While it is possible to perform basic data analysis without specialized tools, harnessing data analytics tools like Python can unlock more profound insights.

In the realm of LIS research, Python's data analysis and visualization capabilities are invaluable. Libraries such as Pandas and NumPy provide powerful tools for manipulating and analyzing datasets, enabling researchers to identify patterns, relationships, and trends within the data. Visualizations created with libraries like Matplotlib and Seaborn aid in effectively communicating research findings, enhancing comprehension and facilitating the discovery of new insights.

Text analysis and natural language processing are also significant areas where Python excels. With the NLTK (Natural Language Toolkit) library, researchers can process and analyze textual data, extract key information, perform sentiment analysis, and even develop language models. These techniques offer powerful ways to uncover patterns and gain deeper insights from large collections of text, such as scholarly articles, social media data, or user feedback.

Additionally, web scraping and data extraction using Python provide researchers with the ability to collect relevant information from websites, online databases, and other web sources. The Beautiful Soup library simplifies the process of parsing and extracting data from HTML or XML documents, while frameworks like Scrapy offer more advanced capabilities for crawling and scraping web pages. This enables researchers to gather data for analysis or track changes in web content, supporting various research objectives, such as studying online information behavior or monitoring trends in digital resources.

By leveraging Python and its associated libraries for data analysis and visualization, text analysis and NLP, as well as web scraping and data extraction, LIS professionals can elevate the quality and depth of their research. The practical examples and techniques explored in this chapter will equip you with the necessary skills to leverage these tools effectively, enabling you to make significant contributions to the field of library and information science and advancing the knowledge and practice of librarianship.

DATA ANALYSIS AND VISUALIZATION

Data analysis and visualization play a critical role in library and information science research, enabling researchers to comprehend and interpret intricate data sets (Katsurai & Joo, 2021). Data analysis involves the systematic examination, cleansing, and organization of data to derive insights and draw conclusions. It encompasses various techniques such as statistical analysis, machine learning, and data mining, facilitating the identification of patterns and relationships within the data.

Visualization, on the other hand, entails the use of graphs, charts, and other visual aids to represent data in a clear and comprehensible manner (Ma & Lund, 2020). Visualizations serve as effective tools for communicating research findings, presenting data in visually appealing formats that are easily understandable. Within library and information science research, data analysis and visualization find numerous applications.

One common application is the identification of patterns and trends in data, such as usage patterns of library resources or borrowing preferences of patrons. This information can inform decisions regarding resource allocation, library services, and can also be employed to test hypotheses and support or refute research questions.

Another key application is the evaluation of the effectiveness of library programs. Through the analysis of data on program attendance and participant satisfaction, researchers can identify the most popular and impactful programs. Visualization tools can then be utilized to present this information to decision-makers, aiding in program planning and resource allocation.

Data analysis and visualization also facilitate the exploration of relationships between library use and other factors, such as age, gender, or socioeconomic status. By analyzing and visualizing these relationships, researchers can gain insights into user demographics and tailor library services accordingly.

Additionally, data analysis and visualization enable the tracking of trends and changes in library usage over time. This facilitates the identification of external factors that may influence library usage patterns, allowing researchers to assess the impact of policies or programs on library usage.

Python offers powerful libraries, including NumPy and Pandas, that are widely used for data analysis and visualization. In this chapter, we will demonstrate the analysis of trends in library user demographics as an example. By understanding changes in user demographics, such as shifts in age, gender, or educational levels over time, researchers can inform library outreach and marketing efforts. Let's consider an example code snippet for analyzing this sample data:

 # Title of Code Sample: Using the Pandas library to conduct data visualization and analysis

 # Objective of Code Sample: The code sample below provides the steps necessary to conduct data visualization and analysis in Python code, using the Pandas library.

Sample Code:

```python
import pandas as pd
#Load the Excel spreadsheet into a Pandas dataframe
df = pd.read_excel('library_users.xlsx')
#Group the data by age and gender and calculate the mean number of visits
visits_by_age_gender = df.groupby(['age', 'gender'])['visits'].mean()
#Calculate the percentage of users in each age group
age_group_percentages = df['age'].value_counts(normalize=True)
```

This script analyzes the data utilizing the Pandas library for data analysis. The data, stored in an Excel spreadsheet, is loaded into a Pandas dataframe using the read_excel() function.

The script then employs the groupby() function to group the data by age and gender, and the mean() function to calculate the average number of visits for each group. The resulting data is stored in the visits_by_age_gender variable and printed to the console, providing the user with the mean number of visits for each group.

Next, the script utilizes the value_counts() function to calculate the percentage of users in each age group. The normalize parameter is set to True, resulting in the counts being normalized to represent percentages. The resulting data is stored in the age_group_percentages variable and printed to the console.

By leveraging the capabilities of Python libraries like Pandas, researchers can effectively analyze and visualize data, enabling them to uncover valuable insights and make informed decisions in the field of library and information science research.

TEXT ANALYSIS AND NATURAL LANGUAGE PROCESSING FOR LIS RESEARCH

While we discussed text analysis in general in the prior chapter, in this section we will focus specifically on text analysis and natural language processing for the purpose of conducting original research in library and information science. Text analysis and natural language processing involve the use of algorithms and computational techniques to analyze and understand text data. These techniques can be used to extract meaning and insights from unstructured text data, such as research articles, book reviews, or social media posts. Text analysis can be used to identify patterns, trends, and relationships within text data, and can be applied to a wide range of research areas, including information retrieval, sentiment analysis, and topic modeling.

Natural language processing is a subfield of text analysis that focuses specifically on the analysis and interpretation of human language. It involves the use of techniques such as language modeling, machine translation, and text classification to understand and analyze text data. Natural language processing can be used to identify the sentiment expressed in text data, classify text into categories, or extract key information from text documents.

There are several Python libraries that can be used for text analysis and natural language processing, such as NLTK (Natural Language Toolkit) and Gensim. These libraries provide tools for tasks such as tokenization, stemming, and part-of-speech tagging, which can be used to preprocess text data for analysis. They also offer advanced techniques such as topic modeling and word embedding, which can be used to uncover patterns and relationships in text data.There are many ways in which text analysis and natural language processing can be used in library and information science research. For example, these techniques can be used to identify trends and patterns in research articles, such as the most common words or phrases used in a particular field, or the most frequently cited authors. Text analysis can also be used to identify relationships between different concepts or ideas, such as the relationship between a particular research topic and the journals in which it is most commonly published.

In addition to these uses, text analysis and natural language processing can be used to support qualitative research, such as content analysis or discourse analysis. These techniques can help researchers to identify themes and patterns in text data, and to explore the meaning and context of words and phrases.

Python has a number of libraries, such as NLTK and Gensim, that can be used to perform text analysis and natural language processing tasks. In this example, we will look at how to retrieve a list of keywords from a document consisting of patron comments:

 # Title of Code Sample: Using the docx library
 # Objective of Code Sample: This code sample demonstrates how to use the docx library in Python code.
 # Sample Code:

```
import docx
import re
```

#Open the Word document

```
document = docx.Document('patron_comments.docx')
```

#Initialize an empty list to store the keywords

```
keywords = []
```

```
#Iterate through each paragraph in the document

for paragraph in document.paragraphs:

#Extract the text of the paragraph

text = paragraph.text

#Use a regular expression to find all the words that are at least three characters long

words = re.findall(r'\b\w{3,}\b', text)

#Add the words to the list of keywords

keywords.extend(words)

#Print the list of keywords

print(keywords)
```

This script uses the docx library to open a Word document and extract the text of each paragraph. The docx library allows the script to work with the structure of the Word document, including paragraphs and styles.

Once the text of each paragraph has been extracted, the script uses a regular expression to find all the words that are at least three characters long. A regular expression is a sequence of characters that forms a search pattern and can be used to match patterns in text. In this case, the regular expression searches for any word that consists of three or more characters and is surrounded by word boundaries. This ensures that the script only matches whole words, rather than parts of words.

The regular expression is used in combination with the findall() function, which searches the text for all occurrences of the pattern and returns a list of the matches. The list of matches is then added to the keywords list using the extend() function. Finally, the script prints the list of keywords to the console. This list can be used for further analysis, such as identifying the most common keywords or exploring relationships between different keywords.

WEB SCRAPING AND DATA EXTRACTION

There are several different methods that can be used for web scraping and data extraction, such as using web scrapers or utilizing web APIs (Application Programming Interfaces). Web scrapers are tools that automatically retrieve and parse data from websites, and can be customized to extract specific types of data, such as text, images, or links. Web APIs, on the other hand, provide a structured way to access and retrieve data from websites, allowing researchers to directly access the data they need without having to parse HTML or other web page elements.

Python offers a range of libraries, such as Beautiful Soup, Selenium, and Requests, that can be used for web scraping and data extraction. These libraries make it easy to write scripts that can extract data from websites and online sources, and can be used to automate data collection processes. Web scraping and data extraction can be a powerful tool for library and information science research, as it allows researchers to gather large amounts of data from the web in an efficient and automated way. However, it is important to be aware of legal and ethical considerations when using these techniques, as some websites may have restrictions on the use of web scrapers or may require permission to access data through APIs.

There are many ways in which web scraping and data extraction can be used in library and information science research. For example, these techniques can be used to collect data from library catalogs or databases, such as the titles and authors of books, the subjects or keywords associated with a particular research topic, or the usage statistics of electronic resources. Web scraping and data extraction can also be used to collect data from social media platforms, such as Twitter or Instagram, or from online news sources.

In addition to collecting data, web scraping and data extraction can also be used to clean and structure data, by removing unwanted characters or formatting the data in a specific way. This can help researchers to prepare data for further analysis, such as data visualization or machine learning.

Python can be used to scrape and extract data from websites and other online sources. This example looks at how to extract book reviews on a specific book from a review website.

The following script first sends a request to the URL of the page with the reviews using the requests library. It then uses the BeautifulSoup library to parse the HTML content of the page and find all the elements with the class "review." Finally, it iterates through each of these elements and extracts the text of the review, which it prints to the console.

Title of Code Sample: How to use the BeautifulSoup library in data extraction
Objective of Code Sample: The following code sample describes the steps involved in using BeautifulSoup to carry out data extraction on the web.
Sample Code:

```
import requests
from bs4 import BeautifulSoup

#URL of the page with the reviews

url = "https://www.goodreads.com/book/show/656.War_and_Peace"
```

```
#Send a request to the URL
response = requests.get(url)
#Parse the HTML content of the page
soup = BeautifulSoup(response.text, 'html.parser')
#Find all the review elements on the page
review_elements = soup.find.all('div', class_='review')
#Iterate through each review element
for element in review_elements:
#Extract the text of the review
review_text = element.find('p').text
#Print the review text
print(review_text)
```

ADDITIONAL CONSIDERATIONS FOR LIS RESEARCH

Ethics and legal considerations are an essential part of working with data science tools in library and information science research. Researchers should be mindful of the privacy and confidentiality of the data they are working with and ensure that they have obtained the necessary permissions and consent to use the data in their research (Elkoumy et al., 2021). This is particularly important when working with sensitive or personal data, such as health records or financial information. Researchers should also be aware of any legal restrictions on the use of data, such as copyright or intellectual property laws. It is important to properly cite any data sources and give credit to the original creators of the data, as this is both a matter of ethical practice and legal requirement. Researchers should also be aware of any terms of service or terms of use agreements that may apply to the data they are working with. These issues will be discussed in further detail in chapter 14 of this book.

Technical limitations and challenges are an important consideration when working with data science tools in library and information science research. Data sets can be large and complex, and may require specialized techniques and hardware to process and analyze. Researchers should be aware of the resources and expertise needed to work with large data sets, and be prepared to invest time and effort in acquiring the necessary skills and tools. Cleaning and preprocessing data is also an important part of the data analysis process. Raw data is often messy and unstructured and requires significant effort to prepare it for analysis (Kaisler et al., 2013). This may involve tasks such as removing missing or invalid values, standardizing data formats, or consolidating data from multiple sources. Researchers should be prepared to spend time cleaning and preprocessing data, as this is an essential step in producing accurate and reliable results. These topics have been discussed in some detail in the earlier chapters of this book. Readers are encouraged to refer back as needed for refreshers on how to prepare data for analysis.

As with all research, it is important for researchers to be aware of the limitations of their analysis when working with data science tools in library and information science research. This includes considering any biases or assumptions that may be present in their data, as these can impact the accuracy and reliability of their results. Researchers should carefully interpret and present their findings and be transparent about any limitations or biases in their data. Researchers should also consider how their findings may be relevant to the larger field of library and information science. This may involve contextualizing their results within the broader literature on the topic, or considering how their findings may inform future research or practice. By considering the broader implications of their work, researchers can contribute to the knowledge and understanding of the field and help to advance the field of library and information science. For more information about how to conduct research in library and information science, there are many great and affordable textbooks available.

REFERENCES

Elkoumy, G., et al. (2021). Privacy and confidentiality in process mining: Threats and research challenges. *ACM Transactions on Management Information System (TMIS), 13*(1), 1-17.

Kaisler, S., Armour, F., Espinosa, J. A., & Money, W. (2013, January). Big data: Issues and challenges moving forward. In *2013 46th Hawaii International Conference on System Sciences* (pp. 995-1004). IEEE.

Katsurai, M., & Joo, S. (2021). Adoption of data mining methods in the discipline of library and information science. *Journal of Library and Information Studies, 19*(1). https://doi.org/10.6182/jlis.202106_19(1).001.

Lund, B. D., & Wang, T. (2021). An analysis of research methods utilized in five top, practitioner-oriented LIS journals from 1980 to 2019. *Journal of Documentation, 77*(5), 1196-208.

Ma, J., & Lund, B. (2020). A cluster analysis of data mining studies in library and information science from 2006 to 2018. *Proceedings of the Association for Information Science and Technology, 57*(1), e413.

Rubin, R. E. (2017). *Foundations of library and information science.* Chicago, IL: American Library Association.

11

Artificial Intelligence Applications

Artificial intelligence (AI) refers to the utilization of computer systems to perform tasks that typically require human intelligence, such as perceiving, synthesizing, and inferring information. It encompasses a wide range of capabilities, including pattern recognition, visual perception, language translation, speech recognition, and decision-making, among others (Russell & Norvig, 2020).

One notable AI development is the advent of ChatGPT, an artificial intelligence chatbot that was launched in November 2022. This powerful AI system has had a profound impact on various fields, eliciting mixed reactions from the public. While some view it as potentially dangerous for humankind and a threat to security, others see it as a revolutionary technology with vast applications (OpenAI, 2022).

The increasing prominence of AI and similar technologies is shaping the future of our world. By emulating human thinking and intelligence, AI can tackle complex problems that were previously beyond the reach of human capabilities. It achieves this by leveraging machine learning and deep learning techniques, enabling intelligent decision-making processes. The applications of AI are virtually limitless, spanning across industries such as e-commerce, education, personal lifestyle, navigation, robotics, healthcare, human resources, agriculture, gaming, automobiles, social media, marketing, chatbots, finance, astronomy, cybersecurity, travel, and transportation (Lund & Wang, 2023).

According to Biswal (2023), the worldwide revenue from the AI software market is projected to reach $126 billion by 2025, with an approximate annual growth rate of 54 percent. Currently, 37 percent of organizations already rely on some form of AI, and the number of enterprises using AI has witnessed a significant growth of 270 percent in the past four years. It is estimated that by 2025, around 95 percent of customer interactions will be driven by AI (Biswal, 2023).

These statistics highlight the accelerating adoption and impact of AI in various sectors, indicating that the future of the world indeed lies in the continued advancement and application of AI and related technologies. As AI continues to evolve, it is crucial for organizations and individuals to adapt and harness its potential to drive innovation, enhance efficiency, and unlock new opportunities in the ever-changing landscape of the digital era.

When it comes to AI, there is often a misconception that it entails the existence of highly intelligent machines or devices surpassing human capabilities and possessing the ability to learn anything. However, this perception is not entirely accurate as we have not reached that level of AI development yet. The true power of AI lies in its capacity to process vast amounts of data and extract valuable insights that may elude human cognition (Raximov et al., 2021).

At the core of AI is machine learning, which involves the ability of a computer program to emulate human intelligence and learn from data or experience. Machine learning combines algorithms, statistical methods, search techniques, and optimization to enable programs to infer patterns or behaviors (Jordan & Mitchell, 2015). Machine learning can be broadly classified into three categories (Mahesh, 2020):

- Supervised machine learning algorithms: These algorithms operate on labeled datasets, where input variables (features or independent variables) are mapped to an output variable (dependent variable or label). Examples of supervised machine learning algorithms include linear and logistic regressions, decision trees, and random forests. For instance, an information professional could employ a regression model using demographic information of patrons and their book checkout history to predict or recommend new books based on individual preferences. Similarly, a decision tree model could help analyze patrons' information needs and behaviors, enabling information professionals to provide tailored and high-quality services.
- Unsupervised machine learning algorithms: These algorithms are utilized when working with unlabeled datasets and are particularly suitable for classification or segmentation purposes. Examples of unsupervised machine learning algorithms include K-means clustering, hierarchical clustering, principal component analysis (PCA), and the a priori algorithm. For instance, library management might aim to identify different categories of library patrons to better understand their specific needs. K-means clustering could assist in achieving this goal by automatically grouping patrons based on their characteristics. This approach avoids the manual segmentation of thousands of patrons and allows information professionals to classify existing customers and predict the needs of future clients.

- Reinforcement learning algorithms: These algorithms learn through trial and error, interacting with their environment to improve decision-making over time. One of the most well-known reinforcement learning algorithms is the Markov Decision Process (MDP). This approach is commonly employed in scenarios where an agent learns from repeated experiences to optimize its actions and maximize rewards.

By leveraging these machine learning algorithms, information professionals can gain valuable insights, make informed decisions, and enhance their services. Whether it's predicting patrons' preferences, segmenting customer groups, or optimizing decision-making processes, machine learning offers a powerful toolset to enhance the capabilities of information management and ensure more efficient and personalized services.

No discussion of AI would be complete without acknowledging the significance of deep learning, a critical component within the field. Deep learning, a subset of machine learning, operates by employing multiple layers of processing to extract meaningful features from vast datasets (LeCun et al., 2015). Its algorithms are particularly prominent in tasks such as image or voice recognition, natural language processing, and speech recognition. Several well-known deep learning algorithms include Convolutional Neural Networks (CNN), Recurrent Neural Networks (RNN), Long Short-Term Memory Networks (LSTMs), Generative Adversarial Networks (GANs), Multilayer Perceptrons (MLPs), Self-Organizing Maps (SOMs), and Radial Basis Function Networks (RBFNs).

In the realm of information retrieval, scholars and professionals have recently introduced neural network techniques to enhance their practices and improve the accuracy of retrieved information. By leveraging deep learning and machine learning algorithms, information professionals can effectively process, organize, transfer, store, and disseminate information. Many online library search programs, database searches, and literature recommendation systems currently rely on some form of machine learning or deep learning algorithms to enhance their functionality. These advancements in AI technologies have set a new trend worldwide, and it is imperative for information professionals to incorporate these algorithms into their processes, programs, and operations.

As AI continues to evolve and shape the field of information management, information professionals stand to benefit greatly from embracing these advanced algorithms. By integrating machine learning and deep learning techniques into their practices, they can streamline workflows, improve the accuracy of information retrieval, enhance user experiences, and unlock valuable insights from vast amounts of data. The adoption of AI algorithms represents a pivotal step toward the future, ensuring that information professionals stay at the forefront of technological advancements and maximize the potential of AI in their domains.

PREDICTING THE NUMBER OF LIBRARIANS NEEDED FOR A LIBRARY

In this use case, we would like to use AI to predict the number of librarians needed for a library based on the population of the covered area, the number of hours opened, the number of regular users of the library, and the total number of annual circulations. The usefulness of AI is its ability to learn from past data and provide guidance or prediction on a future outcome. Managing library resources is paramount for any library operational efficiency, cost, and outstanding customer service; one group of critical staff in library management is librarians. Providing a smaller number of librarians might affect customer service and increase the workload on librarians, which could negatively affect their performance and customer experiences. On the other hand, having too many librarians will increase operational costs and waste resources and money that could sustain other programs for the city or state. The efficient management of librarians is therefore vital for leaderships that oversee library activities. In this example, we will use the dataset about all the libraries in the United States. We have used this dataset in our previous chapter, which is the patrons' dataset. For simplicity, we will only use four features or columns (population of the covered area, number of hours opened, number of regular users of the library, and the total number of annual circulations). The steps needed to accomplish this task are as follows:

1. Import the historic dataset into the development environment;
2. Preprocess the dataset: duplicate, missing values, etc. (in our case, we have a dataset that was preprocessed and ready to use);
3. Split the dataset into training and validation dataset;
4. Develop your model: in this case, we use a linear regression model for simplicity;
5. Train the model and validate the model for accuracy;
6. Import your dataset needed for predicting the number of librarians required for a library;
7. Preprocess the prediction dataset (our prediction dataset is already preprocessed).

Figure 11.1 shows you how to predict the number of librarians needed for each library, along with the outcome of the analysis.

The above example shows that for a covered population of 291,845, a library that needs to open for 10,659 hours per year with an estimated 1,114,668 regular users, and 1,498,017 total annual circulation, the library management should plan for thirty-two librarians for efficient library operations. The above example is a simplistic example of using AI in resource usage prediction for a library operation. Several more complex AI algorithms are out there that an information professional could use to solve advanced information professionals' problems in our field.

Figure 11.1. Prediction of Library Patrons Code and Results
Source: The authors

CATEGORIZING FUTURE LIBRARY RESOURCES BASED ON EXISTING HOLDINGS

In this section, we will discuss how to use Python codes to automate some mundane tasks, especially those tasks that are often done by librarians behind the scenes. Categorization of library resources is one of those many tasks that does not involve direct communication with library patrons. And though it is a critical part of running a library, one would agree that the use of AI tool to categorize library resources has the potential to provide timely, efficient, and even a better experience compared to human categorization. Moreover, this will enable librarians to gain more time focusing on user-centered tasks in the library.

The key to categorizing library resources lies in understanding the various categories that exist in a library holding. Hence, one must understand what type of resources the library holds—series and periodicals, books, reference resources, etc. The format must also be understood. Are all the resources going to be in digital formats or just hard copies? Would there be different formats of the same resource? Answering those questions could help in reducing the amount of Python code to be written, since a good understanding of the resources means that the use of code to categorize future resources would not be too hard to implement. There are different ways of conducting the categorization of library resources with the help of Python codes. One can use Entity Name Recognition to find the right categories based on the title or author of a resource.

Artificial Intelligence Applications

The use of Natural Language Processing Toolkit is a feasible one as well. So, for this example we will keep it simple, succinct, and straight to the point.

Say, you have got a list of resources, with the mixture of books, periodicals, and even journals to categorize. And from the items in the list, figure out what category a resource belongs to. This will come in handle, especially when you like to provide your clienteles and even the library management with a glimpse of resources newly purchased or that already exist in the library holdings.

As with many other use cases of Python code we have shared in this book, the following steps can be used to implement categorization features when it comes to categorizing existing library resources including future ones:

1. First, we need to have the list in a file or represent that list in some suitable data type.
2. Clean the data by following the data preprocessing techniques you have learned from the previous chapter.
3. Apply the appropriate model so you can get the right result.

In this example (Figure 11.2), we will consider having the list of items in a simple data structure called a dictionary. Then create a predefined category for it. This predefined category will then be used to classify items in such a way that having a categorization for existing and future holdings is a breeze. The only challenge here is that for every new item you want to add to be categorized, you would have to manually enter it to the list.

In the provided code snippet, we demonstrated the categorization of the library holdings into two broad categories. However, it is important to note that this was done for the sake of simplicity. Before implementing categorization in your own library, we strongly recommend understanding the specific types

```
--------- Import the python library to use ---------
from collections import defaultdict
--------- create an empty list to hold the list of library resources ---------
resource_categorization = {}
--------- Create the category for your holdings ---------
resource_categorization['periodicals'] = set(['newspapers', 'magazines'])
resource_categorization['reference']   = set(['dictionary', 'bible', 'glossary'])
list_all_resources = set(['newspapers', 'dictionary', 'glossary', 'magaznies', 'books', 'authors'])
resource_items = set.union(*resource_categorization.values())
category = defaultdict(set)
--------- Go through each item in the entire list and assign it to the righ category it belongs to ---------
category['other'] = resource_items.copy()
for key in resource_items.keys():
    category[key] = resource_categorization[key] & items
    category['other'] -= resource_categorization[key]
```

Figure 11.2. Categorization of Materials Code
Source: The authors

of resources present in your library holdings. This understanding will help you determine the most suitable and effective categories to use.

In our example, we opted for a general categorization approach and did not delve into granular details. However, there are additional factors that can be considered for a more detailed categorization. For instance, you could categorize items based on author names, allowing for easy identification and organization of resources by specific authors. Additionally, you could differentiate between digital and physical resources, enabling efficient management of both types within the library system.

The primary objective of implementing categorization through Python code is to create a convenient representation of the library holdings. This representation not only aids in the efficient organization of existing resources but also provides a helpful framework for categorizing future additions to the library. By leveraging code-based categorization techniques, librarians can save time and effort, redirecting their focus towards more user-centered tasks and improving the overall library experience.

THE FUTURE OF AI TECHNOLOGY

Artificial intelligence (AI) has become a game-changer in various industries, including e-commerce, education, healthcare, and finance. Its ability to replicate human intelligence and process vast amounts of data has led to significant advancements. This chapter explores the diverse applications of AI and underscores its importance. Machine learning algorithms, such as supervised, unsupervised, and reinforcement learning, play a crucial role in AI systems. These algorithms enable machines to learn from data and make intelligent decisions. They have immense potential in information management and retrieval.

This chapter highlights the growing significance of AI and its transformative impact on the field of information management. As AI technologies continue to advance, information professionals must stay updated and incorporate these algorithms into their processes and programs. By harnessing the power of AI, they can enhance efficiency, provide better customer experiences, and extract valuable insights from vast amounts of data. Ultimately, AI has the potential to revolutionize the field and propel information management to new heights.

REFERENCES

Biswal, A. (2023). AI applications: Top 18 artificial intelligence applications in 2023. Retrieved from https://www.simplilearn.com/tutorials/artificial-intelligence-tutorial/artificial-intelligence-applications.

Jordan, M. I., & Mitchell, T. M. (2015). Machine learning: Trends, perspectives, and prospects. *Science, 349*(6245), 255–60.

LeCun, Y., Bengio, Y., & Hinton, G. (2015). Deep learning. N*ature, 521*(7553), 436-44.

Lund, B. D., & Wang, T. (2023). Chatting about ChatGPT: How may AI and GPT impact academia and libraries? *Library Hi Tech News, 40*(3), 26-29.

Mahesh, B. (2020). Machine learning algorithms—a review. *International Journal of Science and Research (IJSR), 9*, 381-86.

OpenAI. (2022). Introducing ChatGPT. Retrieved from https://openai.com/blog/chatgpt.

Raximov, N., Primqulov, O., & Daminova, B. (2021). Basic concepts and stages of research development on artificial intelligence. *International Conference on Information Science and Communications Technologies.* https://doi.org/10.1109/ICISCT52966.2021.9670085.

Russell, S., & Norvig, P. (2020). *Artificial intelligence: A modern approach.* Pearson.

Part III

Practical and Ethical Considerations for Using Python

12

Data Explosion, Big Data, and Data Literacy

Throughout this book, we have primarily focused on working with large datasets. For example, the full Institute of Museum and Library Services' Public Library Survey dataset includes almost one million individual pieces of data, or over 5,000 rows and 150 columns. However, these datasets are relatively small compared to those that many data scientists will encounter in their careers. For instance, research data management librarians might work with datasets like the University of Michigan's (2022) Health and Retirement Survey, which collects responses from thousands of questions from older adults across the United States, resulting in tens of millions of data items. Those working with US Census data might have to manage datasets with billions of data items, due to the large population size and the number of questions asked on the decennial survey. It is not possible for the human eye or mind alone to process such large amounts of data, and even standard data software like Microsoft Excel may struggle, as Excel worksheets are limited to 1,048,576 rows of data (Microsoft, 2022).

Big data describes data sets that contain so much data that they cannot be analyzed using traditional means/software. This extends beyond the above examples that involve tens of millions or even billions of data items, into datasets that include trillions or quadrillions of data items. The growth of datasets can escalate rapidly. Consider that right now there are hundreds of millions of active websites in the world, most with multiple web pages (Siteefy, 2022). If you collect data related to content on these web pages (such as with Google's web crawlers), you can easily reach trillions of data items or more. Most large corporations and public entities today will hold big data of some kind. Walmart and Amazon have datasets that include transaction information. Facebook and Twitter have datasets pertaining to users' data. Large universities have datasets covering employee and student server activity.

As mentioned, big data does not always "play nice" with a lot of the standard software you may have used in the past to work with data—software like

Excel or SPSS. In addition to limits in the amount of data that this software can reasonably hold, the amount of processing/computing power required to transform and analyze big datasets often leaves this software frozen, or at least taking an excessive amount of time even to complete simple computations. This situation is where Python really shines. Python can work with terabytes (TBs) of data—trillions of bytes, or x * 8 trillion bits of data—without much of a decrease in performance. This benefit makes Python a requisite skillset for the modern data analyst. An additional benefit of Python for big data is that cleaning, transformation, and analysis require no more work in terms of code than a much smaller dataset, potentially less than twenty lines of code in total.

In this chapter, we will discuss issues concerning the arrival of the data explosion (the emergence of increasing large amounts of data), big data, and data literacy among organizational decision-makers and the general public. Ethical issues will be contemplated alongside practical implementations and guidance for analyzing big data using Python and many of the analytical techniques we have discussed in prior chapters.

THE RAPID INCREASE IN DATA CREATION

Data is generated at a tremendous rate. Research from 2019 suggested that over two exabtyes of data were created each day (Desjardins, 2019). That is 2,000,000,000,000,000,000 bytes, or over 200 million bytes for each person on earth! For comparison, the period at the end of this sentence is a single byte of data. The text file for this chapter is approximately 50 kilobytes of data (50,000 bytes). Consider how much data is generated both actively and passively each day. We post stories on social media, send messages and emails, search Google and create websites that are indexed by the site. We also use wearable devices and generate data like cookies that capture our web usage behavior. It is no surprise that the total data estimated to have been created by 2025 will be over 150 zettabytes (150,000,000,000,000,000,000,000 bytes)!

These numbers are so large that they can be difficult to fully comprehend. It may be helpful to give some more relative measures. According to Bunn (2012), all the academic libraries in the United States together contain about two petabytes of data (2,000,000,000,000,000 bytes). That is a lot of data, no doubt, but only 1/1,000 of the amount of data created each day in the world. That means every bit of data held in U.S. libraries, from the data contained in physical and electronic resources, to metadata, to patron and HR data, still represent a small fraction of the data created *in a single day*. This fact is why there is such great interest in library and information science in tapping into the potential of data science. As librarians, we have the underlying skills of collection and curation, and the "dataverse" represents a huge resource into which we can tap.

The most intriguing and, arguably, important aspect of this data creation, though, is its rapid growth. Recall that two exabytes of data are created each day and that it is expected a total of over 150 zettabytes will have been created by 2025. Well, as of 2010, only two zettabytes of data had ever been created. That means, in a fifteen-year period, seventy-five times more data were expected to be created than had ever been recorded in human history. Whereas Desjardins (2019) suggested that two exabytes of data were created each day in 2019, that number is likely to be much closer to one hundred exabytes by the time you read this book, because the rate of data growth is exponential. Existing sources of data creation (social media, email, trackers, etc.) are not vanishing and new sources of data creation are constantly being developed.

Figure 12.1 shows how the amount of data in existence may continue if the current growth trend persists. As shown in this figure, it is anticipated that the total amount of data would reach one yottabyte (one thousand zettabytes) in late 2034. How many academic libraries would that equal? About one trillion, or enough that each person on earth could have 125 academic research libraries worth of data to themselves!

General Internet data is not the only place where we have experienced tremendous growth. The democratization of the publishing process, owing to platforms like Amazon, has led to a flood of new e-book publications over the past decade. Data collected by Haines (2022) indicates that the number of e-books available via Amazon has increased by an average of 12 percent per year over the past fifteen years. There are over ten million e-books available today, which

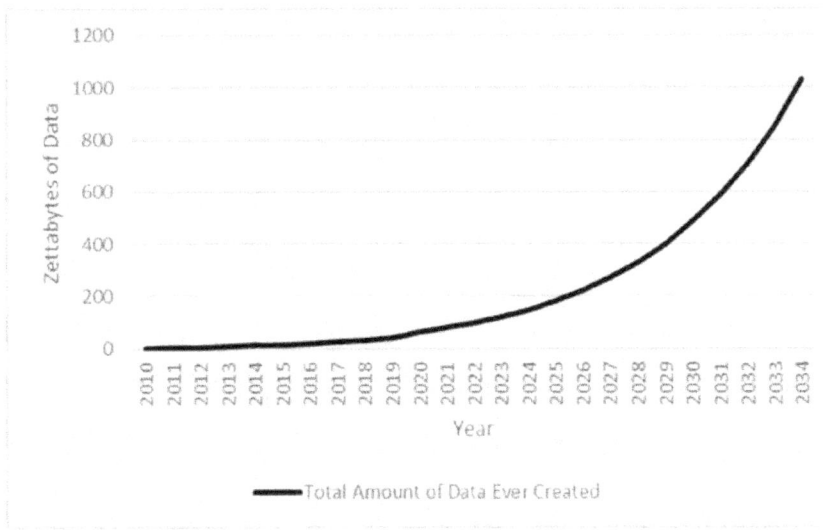

Figure 12.1. Growth in the Amount of Data in the World
Source: The authors

is roughly equal to the total number of unique book titles published from the time of the invention of the printing press (1450) to the start of the twentieth century (Fink-Jensen, 2015). If we consider that the average e-book (including short stories and novellas published as stand-alone publications) is forty thousand words in length, then this means that there are over four hundred billion words published in these books! Consider also the amount of metadata that each of the e-publications requires. The metadata for Kindle Direct Publishing through Amazon may not be as extensive as with most library metadata, but, nonetheless, dozens of fields are required, meaning that if you harvested all this data you would likely have hundreds of millions of bits of data.

Whatever the flavor, the amount of data is only going to increase. Even if the increase in the amount of data created stopped, we would still be creating more data—capturing more behavior data online, publishing more books, recording more audio content—than all of human history pre-1990 combined, on an annual basis! But the growth will not stop. The worldwide population is growing, as is the number of people with reliable Internet access, the number of websites in operation, and the number of widgets and crawlers that collect data. It is nearly unfathomable how much data exists now and is created daily, and it will only become more so in the near future.

WHAT CAN WE DO WITH THIS DATA?

Data by itself does not have inherent value. It is when we do something with the data (whether we are directly doing something or create a machine learning tool that can do it for us) that we can give it value. In order to have data that can be given value and made "information," we need to be able to collect, control, and preserve it, much like with any information product. This is the realm of librarians' expertise. So, do librarians and information professionals have a role in the big data revolution? Most certainly, they will have some role, and they have the potential to claim an even greater one if they work quickly and efficiently to demonstrate their domain expertise.

One task that becomes exponentially more important as the amount of data in a dataset grows is assigning accurate and informative metadata. Consider, for instance, that with a dataset that just consists of one hundred interview question responses, you can read over all of the responses and get a pretty good idea of what the question was. As long as you are relatively accurate in your assessment, you can reestablish the value of this data by adding that header. However, if you have a dataset with one million rows of data, the task is much more difficult. You could read a sample of one hundred rows, but how is one to know whether those rows are truly representative. The feasibility of reading all of the rows in order to make sure you have a complete picture is non-existent, unless you have hundreds of spare hours. The value of this data has thus lost considerable, or even all, value. Now, scale that issue to datasets with tens or hundreds of millions of rows, and consider the wide variety of metadata that is needed to ensure data integrity (that meaning is retained). Librarians addressed this very issue over a century ago when they developed classification systems for reading materials. Certainly, big datasets will be much larger than even the largest library collection, but the principles developed by librarians are translatable to this new context.

Another area where library and information professionals can contribute greatly to big data, and data analytics in general, is through the creation of narratives after data has been analyzed. *Data storytelling* is the creation of narratives that present data findings in a format that is engaging and easily understood by a target audience (Riche et al., 2018). In other words, data storytelling contextualizes data analyses and makes them accessible to the public, much like librarians already do with the information resources they share and provide to the public. They are, to use a bit of a crude metaphor, the "influencers" of the data world. Data storytelling does require some technical knowledge of the analyses performed, but mostly relies on the ability of the storyteller to present the findings in a way that has authenticity and authority. The area of data storytelling is a relatively young field/profession, with ample growth anticipated on the horizon.

A final example of an area in big data analytics where library and information professionals can have a major role is with needs analysis. Needs analysis is one of the foundational service models of librarianship (Greer et al., 2013), as well as a critical component of most systems design models (Stair & Reynolds, 2017). It involves the identification of the actual needs of a user and/or the requirements necessary to address those needs, often through the use of data analysis, observation, and interviews. This type of role could become crucial in the big data era in order to ensure that the data being collected and analyses being performed are valuable and that time and resources/computing power are not wasted on data that is analyzed without any real purpose or value.

Of course, these are just three of many examples of roles that librarians could take in the era of big data. Certainly, library and information professionals may be involved in doing analyses themselves, or overseeing analyses performed by a team of analysts (Semeler et al., 2019). The versatility of the library and information professional's skillset, including soft skills and technical skills, suits them well for a variety of roles.

EXAMPLE OF BIG DATASETS

There are many examples of big datasets that can be found online and used for experimentation or novel analysis. Government sources (see Data.gov below) are always good sources, because of the data quality standards that are usually followed. However, non-profits and advertiser platforms also often collect a lot of data, and some make this data (or at least outdated versions of it) available to the public. The following are four data sources that you might find useful if you are interested in getting some practice with analyzing large datasets yourself. Keep in mind that GitHub also has many great datasets, it just may take a bit more parsing to find them compared to these other platforms.

Yahoo! Research offers the Webscope datasets for registered users with an .edu email address. New datasets are constantly added. The datasets are sorted into six main categories: Advertising and Market Data, which includes data related to web marketing projects; Computing Systems Data, which tracks accesses to the Yahoo! databases; Language Data, which includes data related to Yahoo! searches and queries posted to Yahoo! Answers; Competition Data, which includes datasets specifically used for improving existing machine learning algorithms; Graph and Social Data, which includes data that relates to spatial and topical mapping; and Ratings and Classification Data, which includes data relating to user reviews on platforms like Yahoo! Music and Yahoo! Movies. Available at https://webscope.sandbox.yahoo.com/.

AWS (Amazon Web Services) has an open data repository, which includes data from Amazon as well as registered affiliates, including many universities and other non-profits. AWS actually uses GitHub to provide access to data. Its primary benefit is that it provides easy access and an overview of relevant and trustworthy datasets. The AWS open data service is particularly useful for those interested in biomedicine and geography; however, datasets related to a variety of topics are available. Available at https://aws.amazon.com/opendata/.

Stanford University's Stanford Network Analysis Project (SNAP) offers the Stanford Large Network Dataset Collection for all users. The datasets are varied, covering social media networks, citation networks, research collaboration networks, product purchasing networks, system use networks, and physical geography networks, among others. Generally, these datasets have originated as part of an ongoing research project. Not all of the included datasets qualify as big datasets, but they can make useful data for testing out various analytical approaches nonetheless. Available at http://snap.stanford.edu/.

Data.gov holds a wide variety of big datasets that were collected/created on behalf of the United States government and are available to all users. This repository was a key component of the eGovernment initiatives in the United States during the early 2000s. Here, you can find data related to commerce, defense, and education, as well as the U.S. Census. This collection includes thousands of big datasets with millions of data items and hundreds of thousands of datasets overall. The datasets are generally available in multiple formats, including csv, xml, and xls. Available at https://data.gov/.

WHAT'S NEXT FOR BIG DATA?

Because the amount of data created will only continue to increase—barring some Y2K or global ecological catastrophe—the need for big data analytics will also continue to grow. Python is a robust coding language that allows for the handling and analysis of big data. This situates it well for future growth of data science. One issue that we can anticipate, and for which Python is well-prepared, is refinements to the ways that data are currently cleaned/processed and analyzed. For a long time, the major ways of doing things in data science have remained relatively the same, in no small part because the same people/type of people have adopted the roles of computer scientists and data analysts. However, data science as a profession and field of research is becoming increasingly more diverse while simultaneously experiencing substantial growth (Daniel, 2019). If one looks to any other profession/field that has experienced similar change, such as within higher education in the 2000s, you will find that a range of new ideas and philosophies emerge in an area that was previously characterized by stagnation.

Data analysts should also be prepared for huge amounts of data that can be harnessed and analyzed in real time in order to respond to active needs or trends. Consider, for instance, that you have an algorithm that dynamically calculates the price of admission to a theme park based on factors like the number of current guests, weather conditions, and time of day. This probably is not a scenario that most readers would like to see in the future, but is nonetheless one that is highly probably, and it will be the data scientists' jobs to design the types of algorithms that can constantly update cost-value (like with the stock market) as new data is continuously inputted. This principle of predicting human behavior and adjusting the price one will pay/charge dynamically based on this prediction has long been fundamental to markets, where these concepts are fundamental to investment strategy (Niederhoffer & Osborne, 1966). If this becomes a reality in other areas of life, Python is well-situated to handle the task.

Although there are many unknowns about the future of big data, one thing is certain: the principles of Python and data analysis outlined in this book provide a solid foundation for tackling any future challenges. These principles are scalable, meaning they can be applied to data of any size and format. Additionally, the Python development and support teams ensure that the language stays current and relevant in the face of changing data environments, automation, and other aspects of the fourth industrial revolution.

REFERENCES

Bunn, J. (2012). *How big is a petabyte, exabyte, zettabyte, or a yottabyte?* Retrieved from http://highscalability.com/blog/2012/9/11/how-big-is-a-petabyte-exabyte-zettabyte-or-a-yottabyte.html.

Daniel, B. K. (2019). Big data and data science: A critical review of issues for educational research. *British Journal of Educational Technology, 50*(1), 101–13.

Desjardins, J. (2019, April). How much data is generated each day? *World Economic Forum.* Retrieved from https://www.weforum.org/agenda/2019/04/how-much-data-is-generated-each-day-cf4bddf29f/.

Fink-Jensen, J. (2015). *Book titles per capita*. Retrieved from https://datasets.iisg.amsterdam/dataset.xhtml?persistentId=hdl:10622/AOQMAZ.

Greer, R. C., Grover, R. J., & Fowler, S. G. (2013). *Introduction to the library and information professions* (2nd edition). Santa Barbara, CA: Libraries Unlimited.

Haines, D. (2022). *There are now well over 12 million Kindle ebooks on the Amazon store*. Retrieved from https://justpublishingadvice.com/there-are-now-over-5-million-kindle-ebooks/.

Microsoft. (2022). Excel specifications and limits. Retrieved from https://support.microsoft.com/en-us/office/excel-specifications-and-limits-1672b34d-7043-467e-8e27-269d656771c3.

Niederhoffer, V., & Osborne, M. F. (1966). Market making and reversal on the stock exchange. *Journal of the American Statistical Association, 61*(316), 897–916.

Riche, N. H., Hurter, C., Diakopoulos, N., & Carpendale, S. (2018). *Data-driven storytelling*. Boca Raton, FL: CRC Press.

Semeler, A. R., Pinto, A. L., & Rozados, H. B. (2019). Data science in data librarianship: Core competencies of a data librarian. *Journal of Librarianship and Information Science, 51*(3), 771–80.

Siteefy. (2022). *How many websites are there in the world?* Retrieved from https://siteefy.com/how-many-websites-are-there/.

Stair, R., & Reynolds, G. (2017). *Principles of information systems*. Boston, MA: Cengage Learning.

University of Michigan. (2022). *Health and retirement study*. Retrieved from https://hrs.isr.umich.edu/about.

13
Data Ethics

Data ethics is a critical aspect of working with data. It involves ensuring that data is collected, used, and shared in a way that is responsible, ethical, and transparent, and that it is protected from unauthorized access or misuse. This is particularly important given the sensitive nature of many types of data, and the potential for data to be misused or exploited in ways that could harm individuals or society. Some key concepts related to data ethics include data privacy and confidentiality, data accuracy and reliability, data bias and fairness, and data governance. Ensuring that these issues are properly addressed is essential in order to build trust in data and to ensure that data is used in a way that is beneficial to society. This is especially important given the increasing reliance on data in many aspects of our lives, from business and policy decision-making to personal decision-making and interactions with others. Data ethics requires a commitment to transparency, accountability, and continuous learning, in order to ensure that data is used in a way that respects the rights and interests of individuals and society. In this chapter, we will discuss these ethical issues in detail.

DATA PRIVACY AND CONFIDENTIALITY

Privacy and confidentiality are core values of librarianship and are essential to building trust with patrons and protecting the integrity of the library's collections and services (Cooke, 2018). These values should also be applied to working with data, as handling data responsibly helps to ensure that sensitive information is protected and that individuals' privacy is respected. This is particularly important in today's digital age, where vast amounts of data are collected and shared online (Mehta & Wang, 2020). Librarians have a professional obligation to uphold the principles of privacy and confidentiality when working with data and should take steps to ensure that any data they handle is handled securely and with respect for the rights of individuals.

It is essential to ensure that personal and sensitive data is protected and not disclosed to unauthorized individuals or organizations. This includes following relevant laws and regulations, such as the General Data Protection Regulation (GDPR) in Europe and the Health Insurance Portability and Accountability Act (HIPAA) in the United States. Data analysis can be a threat in the face of GDPR and HIPAA regulations due to the sensitive nature of the data that is often being analyzed (Kalkman et al., 2022). Both GDPR and HIPAA are designed to protect the privacy and security of personal data, and they impose strict requirements on organizations that handle such data.

Under GDPR, personal data is defined as any information relating to an identified or identifiable natural person (Goddard, 2017). This includes information such as names, addresses, phone numbers, and email addresses, as well as more sensitive information such as health data and financial information. GDPR requires that organizations that collect, use, or store personal data must do so in a way that is lawful, fair, and transparent, and must have a legitimate reason for doing so.

HIPAA is a similar set of regulations that applies specifically to the healthcare industry. It establishes standards for the protection of personal health information (PHI) that is transmitted or maintained by covered entities (such as hospitals and healthcare providers) and their business associates (Annas, 2003). HIPAA requires that PHI be kept secure and confidential, and that it only be used or disclosed for authorized purposes.

In the context of data analysis, the threat comes from the fact that data analysis often involves the collection, storage, and processing of large amounts of personal data. If this data is not handled in accordance with GDPR or HIPAA requirements, it could potentially be misused or exposed, leading to privacy breaches and legal consequences for the organization (Talesh, 2018). Therefore, it is important for organizations that engage in data analysis to be aware of and comply with these regulations, to protect the privacy and security of personal data.

DATA SECURITY

Ensuring the security of data is crucial, as data breaches can have significant consequences for individuals and organizations. Library professionals should take steps to protect data from unauthorized access, such as through encryption and secure storage and transmission. Data security is an important aspect of data ethics, as it pertains to the protection of personal and sensitive information from unauthorized access or misuse (Tankard, 2012). Data security is a threat for data ethics because it is essential for protecting the privacy and confidentiality of individuals, and for ensuring that data is used in a responsible and ethical manner.

There are several different threats to data security that can pose risks to data ethics. Some examples of these threats include:

- Cyberattacks: Cyberattacks are a common threat to data security, and can involve the unauthorized access or theft of sensitive data. Cyberattacks can be carried out by hackers or other malicious actors, and can have serious consequences for individuals and organizations (Agrafiotis et al., 2018).
- Data breaches: A data breach is an incident in which sensitive data is accessed or disclosed without authorization. Data breaches can occur due to a variety of reasons, such as human error, system vulnerabilities, or malicious attacks (Kolevski & Michael, 2015).
- Data misuse: Data misuse occurs when data is used for purposes other than those for which it was collected, or in a way that is not consistent with ethical principles. Data misuse can have serious consequences for individuals, and can erode trust in the organizations that collect and use data (Shabtai et al., 2014).
- Insufficient data protection measures: Inadequate data protection measures can also pose a threat to data security. This can include a lack of encryption, inadequate access controls, or a lack of awareness about data security best practices.

Overall, the threat of data security for data ethics is particularly important in the context of libraries. Libraries collect and store vast amounts of data, including personal information about their patrons, and have a professional obligation to protect the privacy and confidentiality of this information (Lund, 2021). This means taking appropriate measures to secure the data they hold and ensure that it is used in a responsible and ethical manner. By upholding their ethical responsibilities in relation to data security, libraries can build trust with their patrons and protect the integrity of their collections and services.

DATA ACCURACY AND RELIABILITY

It is important to ensure that data is accurate and reliable, as errors or biases in data can lead to flawed or misleading conclusions (Barchard & Pace, 2011). Library professionals should be diligent in checking the quality of their data sources and verifying the accuracy of their data analysis. Data accuracy and reliability are important for data ethics because they ensure that the data being used is accurate and trustworthy. When data is accurate, it means that it is free from errors and represents the true state of affairs (Fox et al., 1994). When data is reliable, it means that it can be trusted to be consistent and dependable.

The importance of data accuracy and reliability for data ethics becomes clear when you consider the potential consequences of using incorrect or unreliable data. If data is inaccurate or unreliable, it can lead to flawed conclusions and decisions, which can have serious consequences for individuals and society (Graves et al., 2016). For example, if data is used to make policy decisions or allocate resources, and that data is incorrect or unreliable, it could result in resources being misallocated or policies being implemented that are not effective. This could cripple a library that already faces budget constraints.

In addition, using inaccurate or unreliable data can also erode trust in the data and the organizations that use it (Medeiros, 2013). When people lose trust in the data being used, they may be less likely to believe or act on the conclusions or recommendations that are based on that data. This can have negative consequences for society, as it can lead to a breakdown in trust and cooperation.

DATA OWNERSHIP AND CONSENT

It is important to ensure that data is collected and used with the appropriate consent and in compliance with relevant laws and regulations. This includes obtaining consent from individuals for the collection and use of their personal data and respecting the intellectual property rights of data creators. The issue of consent is an important aspect of data ethics when using Python or any other programming language for data analysis. Consent refers to the process of obtaining permission from individuals before collecting, using, or sharing their personal data (Crow et al., 2006).

In the context of data ethics, obtaining consent is important because it helps to ensure that individuals are aware of how their data is being used, and that they have the opportunity to opt in or opt out of having their data collected or used (Purcaru et al., 2014). This is particularly important when it comes to sensitive personal data, such as health information or financial information, which may be more sensitive and require greater protection. Obtaining consent is also important because it helps to build trust between individuals and organizations (Rennie, 1997). When individuals feel that their data is being handled responsibly and ethically, they are more likely to trust the organization and be willing to share their data.

In terms of using Python or any other programming language for data analysis, obtaining consent is important because it ensures that the data being analyzed is being used in a responsible and ethical manner. This may involve obtaining explicit consent from individuals before collecting their data or providing individuals with the opportunity to opt out of having their data collected or used. It may also involve taking steps to ensure that the data is handled securely and confidentially, and that it is only used for the purposes for which it was collected.

DATA TRANSPARENCY AND ACCOUNTABILITY

Library professionals should be transparent about their data collection and analysis practices and be willing to account for any errors or limitations in their work. This helps to ensure that the data is used ethically and responsibly, and that any conclusions drawn from it are trustworthy. Data transparency and accountability are important for data ethics because they help to ensure that data is being used in a responsible and ethical manner (Bertino et al., 2019). Data transparency refers to the idea that data should be open and accessible, and that individuals should be able to understand how their data is being used. Data accountability refers to the idea that organizations that collect and use data should be held accountable for their actions, and that they should be responsible for ensuring that data is used in a responsible and ethical manner (Ko, 2014).

The importance of data transparency and accountability for data ethics becomes clear when you consider the potential consequences of using data in an irresponsible or unethical manner. If data is not used transparently or accountability is not exercised, it can lead to flawed conclusions and decisions, which can have serious consequences for an organization. For example, if data is used to make policy decisions or allocate resources, and that data is not used transparently or accountability is not exercised, it could result in resources being misallocated or policies being implemented that are not effective (Hora et al., 2017).

In addition, a lack of data transparency and accountability can also erode trust in the data and the organizations that use it. When people lose trust in the data being used, they may be less likely to believe or act on the conclusions or recommendations that are based on that data. This can have negative consequences for society, as it can lead to a breakdown in trust and cooperation.

EXTREME AUTOMATION

There is the potential that languages like Python can be used to create overpowering AI. One example is a platform like ChatGPT. Extreme automation through platforms like ChatGPT can present a number of risks, including:

- "Inaccurate or biased output: One risk of extreme automation is that the output of the platform may be inaccurate or biased. This can occur if the data used to train the platform is not representative or is biased in some way. As a result, the output of the platform may not accurately reflect reality or may be biased in favor of certain groups or perspectives.
- "Dependence on the platform: Another risk of extreme automation is that it can lead to a dependence on the platform. This can be problematic if the platform is not reliable or if it goes offline, as it can disrupt the functioning of the systems that rely on it.

- "Loss of jobs: Extreme automation through platforms like ChatGPT can also lead to the loss of jobs, as it can replace human labor with machine labor. This can have negative consequences for workers and communities, particularly if alternative employment opportunities are not available.
- "Ethical concerns: Extreme automation can also raise ethical concerns, such as the question of whether it is appropriate to rely on machines to make decisions that can have significant impacts on people's lives. This is particularly relevant in fields such as healthcare and criminal justice, where the consequences of error can be severe" (OpenAI, 2022).

One of the most concerning aspects of a platform like ChatGPT is that it is difficult, if not impossible, to tell that you are interacting with an AI platform rather than a real human being. Famously, the Turing test (named after Alan Turing) is a measure used to examine whether a human user can distinguish their interactions between an AI interface and a human user. Think AI could never be that advanced? The four bullet points above were written entirely by an AI program (https://chat.openai.com/). Could you tell?

The good news? Even ChatGPT does not believe that it will replace the roles of professional librarians:

"It is unlikely that ChatGPT or any other artificial intelligence (AI) platform will completely eliminate the need for professional librarians. While AI and other technologies can automate certain tasks and functions, there are many aspects of librarianship that require human judgment and expertise.

"For example, librarians are trained professionals who are skilled at organizing and managing information, and they play a critical role in providing access to information resources. They are also skilled at helping people find and use information, and they often work closely with researchers and other users to identify and meet their information needs.

"AI and other technologies may be able to automate certain tasks related to these activities, such as cataloging and classification, but they are unlikely to completely replace the expertise and judgment of professional librarians.

"In addition, librarians also play important roles in areas such as collection development, preservation, and outreach, which may be difficult or impossible for AI and other technologies to replicate" (OpenAI, 2022).

At the time of this writing, ChatGPT is still in its testing phase and is available only to researchers through https://chat.openai.com/chat. The power of these platforms is undeniable and is possible to replicate through the types of machine learning concepts we discuss in this book (though the scale of these tools is far beyond what we discuss in this book). There are other questions about ChatGPT, such as who owns the copyright for responses, which have not yet been satisfactorily answered at the time of this writing (Floridi & Chiriatti,

2020). For the sake of covering our bases, we have included the text written by ChatGPT in quotation marks and provided the attribution above.

PREPARING FOR ETHICAL CHALLENGES

Data ethics is a complex and multifaceted issue that requires careful consideration and planning in order to ensure that data is collected, used, and shared in a responsible and ethical manner. Some key challenges related to data ethics include data privacy and confidentiality, data accuracy and reliability, data bias and fairness, and data governance. To prepare for these ethical challenges, it is important to be aware of the relevant laws, regulations, and best practices that apply to the collection and use of data, and to have processes in place to ensure that these requirements are met. This may involve implementing policies, procedures, and controls to protect personal and sensitive data, and to ensure that data is accurate, reliable, and free from bias. It may also involve establishing clear roles, responsibilities, and processes for managing data, and for addressing any ethical issues that may arise. By being proactive in addressing these challenges, organizations can help to build trust in data, and to ensure that data is used in a way that is ethical, transparent, and beneficial to society.

REFERENCES

Agrafiotis, I., Nurse, J. R., Goldsmith, M., Creese, S., & Upton, D. (2018). A taxonomy of cyber-harms: Defining the impacts of cyber-attacks and understanding how they propagate. *Journal of Cybersecurity, 4*(1).

Annas, G. J. (2003). HIPAA regulations: A new era of medical-record privacy? *New England Journal of Medicine, 348*, 1486–90.

Barchard, K. A., & Pace, L. A. (2011). Preventing human error: The impact of data entry methods on data accuracy and statistical results. *Computers in Human Behavior, 27*(5), 1834–39.

Bertino, E., Merrill, S., Nesen, A., & Utz, C. (2019). Redefining data transparency: A multidimensional approach. *Computer, 52*(1), 16–26.

Cooke, L. (2018). Privacy, libraries and the era of big data. *IFLA Journal, 44*(3), 167–69.

Crow, G., Wiles, R., Heath, S., & Charles, V. (2006). Research ethics and data quality: The implications of informed consent. *International Journal of Social Research Methodology, 9*(2), 83–95.

Floridi, L., & Chiriatti, M. (2020). GPT-3: Its nature, scope, limits, and consequences. *Minds and Machines, 30*(4), 681–94.

Fox, C., Levitin, A., & Redman, T. (1994). The notion of data and its quality dimensions. *Information Processing & Management, 30*(1), 9–19.

Goddard, M. (2017). The EU General Data Protection Regulation (GDPR): European regulation that has a global impact. *International Journal of Market Research, 59*(6), 703-05.

Graves, J. T., Acquisti, A., & Christin, N. (2016). Big data and bad data: On the sensitivity of security policy to imperfect information. *University of Chicago Law Review, 83*, 117.

Hora, M. T., Bouwma-Gearhart, J., & Park, H. J. (2017). Data driven decision-making in the era of accountability: Fostering faculty data cultures for learning. *The Review of Higher Education, 40*(3), 391-426.

Kalkman, S., van Delden, J., Banerjee, A., Tyl, B., Mostert, M., & van Thiel, G. (2022). Patients' and public views and attitudes towards the sharing of health data for research: A narrative review of the empirical evidence. *Journal of Medical Ethics, 48*(1), 3-13.

Ko, R.K.L. (2014). Data accountability in cloud systems. In S. Nepal & M. Pathan (Eds.), *Security, privacy and trust in cloud systems* (pp. 211-38). Berlin, Heidelberg: Springer.

Kolevski, D., & Michael, K. (2015, October). Cloud computing data breaches a socio-technical review of literature. In *2015 International Conference on Green Computing and Internet of Things (ICGCIoT)* (pp. 1486-95). IEEE.

Lund, B. D. (2021). Public libraries' data privacy policies: A content and cluster analysis. *The Serials Librarian, 81*(1), 99-107.

Medeiros, N. (2013). A public trust: Libraries and data curation. *OCLC Systems & Services, 29*(4), 192-94.

Mehta, D., & Wang, X. (2020). COVID-19 and digital library services: A case study of a university library. *Digital Library Perspectives, 36*(4), 351-63.

OpenAI. (2022). ChatGPT. Retrieved from https://chat.openai.com/chat.

Purcaru, D., Preda, A., Popa, D., Moga, M. A., & Rogozea, L. (2014). Informed consent: How much awareness is there? *PloS One, 9*(10), e110139.

Rennie, D. (1997). Disclosure to the reader of institutional review board approval and informed consent. *JAMA, 277*(11), 922-23.

Shabtai, A., Bercovitch, M., Rokach, L., & Elovici, Y. (2014). Optimizing data misuse detection. *ACM Transactions on Knowledge Discovery from Data (TKDD), 8*(3), 1-23.

Talesh, S. A. (2018). Data breach, privacy, and cyber insurance: How insurance companies act as "compliance managers" for businesses. *Law & Social Inquiry, 43*(2), 417-40.

Tankard, C. (2012). Big data security. *Network security, 2012*(7), 5-8.

14

Knowledge and Data Economy

Data science is a rapidly growing field with significant economic value. As data becomes increasingly important in various industries—including many in which LIS professionals are employed (e.g., higher education, knowledge management)—understanding the economic implications of data and data science is essential. In this chapter, we will explore some of the key issues related to the economic value of data and data science, including data ownership, data quality, and data monopolies. We will also discuss the role of data librarianship in managing and organizing data collections, and the increasing demand for data librarians as more organizations recognize the importance of managing and using data effectively. Finally, we will consider the economic value of data literacy and the importance of educating and training individuals to be proficient in working with data. Understanding these issues is essential for anyone interested in the economic value of data and data science and can help individuals and organizations to make informed decisions about data management and use.

THE ECONOMICS OF DATA

Data has immense value. It has this value because it can provide insights, inform decision-making, and drive progress. It can help businesses make better decisions by providing information on customer behavior, market trends, and other relevant factors (Khade, 2016). In the healthcare industry, data can be used to improve patient care and outcomes, as well as to identify trends and patterns that can inform the development of new treatments and therapies (Stead & Lorenzi, 1999). In the public sector, data can be used to inform policy decisions, allocate resources more effectively, and measure the impact of programs and initiatives. Data has the potential to revolutionize industries and transform the way we live and work. The monetary value of data carries both opportunities and risks that should be explored.

DATA OWNERSHIP

The concept of data ownership is a significant factor in determining the economic value of data. It refers to the legal rights and responsibilities related to the control, possession, and usage of data (Al-Khouri, 2012). Sometimes the individual who creates the data owns it, such as when a person shares personal information on social media. In these instances, the individual maintains ownership of their data and has the right to control how it is utilized. However, in some cases, such as with social media, rights to the data can be relinquished or granted to other entities, possibly as a requirement for using a platform (Small et al., 2012). In other instances, the organization that collects the data owns it, such as when a company gathers customer data through a loyalty program. In these situations, the company has the legal right to use and control the data, as it was collected as part of the company's business operations (Fadler & Legner, 2022). Customers can choose not to participate in the program, but those who do agree to participate have no legal claim over the data if the company collects and uses it in accordance with its policies.

The issue of data ownership can have significant economic consequences, as data can be a valuable asset that can be bought and sold (Nolin, 2020). Companies may acquire data from other organizations or individuals in order to gain insights or to use it for marketing purposes. There are numerous services that specialize in facilitating data exchange (Amado et al., 2018). On the other hand, individuals or organizations may also sell their data to other companies or organizations in return for payment. The ability to buy and sell data has led to the creation of a data economy, where data is treated as a tradable commodity, like a barrel of oil (Nolin, 2020). The topic of data ownership can be complex and may differ depending on the context and legal jurisdiction. For instance, laws surrounding data ownership may vary from one country to another, and there may be conflicting legal opinions on who has the right to own and control data (Hummel et al., 2021). Countries in the European Union generally have strong, cohesive protections for consumers in regards to data ownership, while some countries in the Global South may have very few consumer protections (Hoofnagle et al., 2019). Therefore, it is important for individuals and organizations to be aware of the legal and ethical considerations of data ownership and to take these matters into account when handling data.

DATA QUALITY

Data quality is an essential aspect to consider when making decisions or drawing conclusions based on data. Inaccurate or poor quality data can result in flawed conclusions or decisions, which can have economic consequences (Lee et al., 2006). This is particularly relevant in industries such as finance and healthcare, where accurate data is crucial. In finance, for instance, low quality data can lead to incorrect risk assessments or investment decisions, which can result in financial losses for individuals or organizations (Tee et al., 2007). Many large financial organizations operate on narrow profit margins, where the difference between millions in profit and millions in losses is significant. As such, poor quality data can be a significant concern that could potentially cause a financial collapse.In the healthcare industry, low quality data can result in misdiagnoses or incorrect treatments, which can have serious consequences for patients (Orfanidis et al., 2004). It can also cause inefficiencies and higher costs for healthcare organizations. Moreover, poor quality data can lead to significant legal issues if data under the control of a healthcare organization is ever corrupted or compromised in a way that violates federal laws or damages patient trust. These issues could lead to a loss of patients or, even worse, a major lawsuit. Ensuring the quality of data is therefore important for both individual and organizational decision-making. This can involve processes such as data cleansing, validation, and verification to ensure that the data is accurate, complete, and relevant (Chen, 2022). It is also important to have systems in place to monitor and maintain data quality over time.

DATA MONOPOLIES

Another issue related to the economic value of data is the risk of data monopolies. A monopoly is a market structure in which a single firm is the sole supplier of a particular product or service (Lerner, 1934). In a monopoly, the firm has complete control over the price of the product or service, as there are no other firms offering a substitute. Monopolies can arise in a number of ways, including through government grants of exclusive rights to a firm, through natural barriers to entry that prevent other firms from entering the market, or through the acquisition of all other firms in the market by a single firm. A data monopoly occurs when a single company or organization controls a large amount of data and is able to use it to dominate a particular market (Ma, 2022). Some companies have already attained a status that could be considered a near-monopoly, such as Google, which benefits from having about 90 percent of the world's online searches. Google does not necessarily "sell" users data, but it does not need to—it can use the data itself to ensure further success.Data monopolies can have a number of negative consequences, including:

Lack of competition: Data monopolies can limit competition in a particular market, as the company or organization with the monopoly has an advantage over its competitors due to its access to large amounts of data (Stucke & Grunes, 2016). This can lead to higher prices and less innovation, as other companies may be unable to compete effectively.
Privacy concerns: Data monopolies can also raise privacy concerns, as the company or organization with the monopoly may have access to a large amount

of personal data (Acquisti et al., 2016). This can raise concerns about how the data is being used and whether individuals' privacy is being respected.

Lack of transparency: Data monopolies may also be less transparent about how they are using data, as they may have less incentive to disclose this information (Kerber, 2016). This can make it difficult for individuals and regulators to understand how the data is being used and to ensure that it is being used responsibly.

Direct economic consequences: Data monopolies can also have direct economic consequences, as they may lead to higher prices and reduced competition (Loertscher & Marx, 2020). This can have negative effects on consumers and businesses, and it may limit economic growth in a particular market.

Like traditional monopolies, data monopolies can be challenging to dismantle because the companies that attain this status often have significant control and influence (Lamoreaux, 2019). This can include grant funding, internships, and other partnerships with universities. These resources and connections can help the company maintain its dominant position in the market, making it difficult for other companies to compete. Additionally, data monopolies may have the financial resources to engage in lobbying and other efforts to shape public policy and public opinion in their favor.

DATA LIBRARIANSHIP

The emergence of a data-driven economy has transformed traditional roles within the library and information professions as well. One of the new roles that has emerged in recent years is that of the data librarian (Khan & Du, 2018). Many of those reading this book now may have their own eyes set on such a role. This role combines traditional library tasks with data science and management tasks, where the librarians serve a key role in supporting the research data management needs of a university.

Data librarians are professionals who are responsible for managing and organizing data collections and assisting users in finding, accessing, and using data (Semeler et al., 2019). They may work in a variety of settings, including academic libraries, government agencies, and private organizations. To be a data librarian, one often needs to have advanced degrees in library science or a related field, and one may also have specialized training in data management or data science.

The role of a data librarian involves a range of activities, including acquiring and cataloging data, developing data management plans, and providing data literacy education and training (Koltay, 2017). The demand for data librarians is increasing as more organizations recognize the importance of managing and using data effectively. Data librarians may have the opportunity to work with a wide range of data types and formats, including statistical data, geospatial data, and scientific data.

Data librarians often work closely with researchers, policy-makers, and other stakeholders to support data-driven decision-making and research (Federer, 2018). They may also be involved in promoting data sharing and open data initiatives and may work to ensure that data is preserved for future use. Overall, the role of a data librarian is crucial in helping organizations effectively use and manage data to make informed decisions and drive research and innovation.

It is difficult to estimate an exact salary range for data librarians, as salaries can vary widely depending on a number of factors, including the location, type of organization, and level of experience of the data librarian. According to salary data from the website Glassdoor (2022), data librarians at academic institutions in the United States may earn an average salary of around $60,000 per year, while data librarians at government agencies may earn an average salary of around $70,000 per year. However, these figures are merely estimates.

Beyond the data librarian position, are many alternative careers for individuals trained both in librarianship and data science, making this a worthwhile educational pairing to pursue. They also tend to be quite lucrative financially for the professional. These positions include:

- **Data scientists** use their skills in statistics and programming to analyze and interpret large datasets (Davenport & Patil, 2012). They may work in a variety of industries, such as finance, healthcare, or technology, and may use their expertise in data science to help improve health outcomes in the field of health informatics (Meyer, 2019). Data scientists often work with large amounts of data, using techniques such as machine learning and data mining to extract insights and inform decision-making. They may also be involved in developing data-driven products or solutions, and may work closely with other stakeholders, such as business analysts and data engineers. The demand for data scientists is high as organizations increasingly recognize the value of data-driven decision-making and insights.
- **Information architects** design and organize information systems and structures. They may work in a variety of industries, such as library and information science, information technology, or consulting, and are responsible for creating logical and intuitive ways to organize and present information (Morville, 2021). Information architects often work with complex information systems and may use techniques such as user experience (UX) design and data visualization to create user-friendly interfaces and data products. They may also be involved in the development of information governance and management policies, and may work with stakeholders such as librarians, data scientists, and business analysts to ensure that information is properly structured and maintained.

- **Data analysts** collect, process, and analyze large datasets. They may work in a variety of industries, such as finance, healthcare, or marketing, and are responsible for extracting insights and trends from data. Data analysts often work with large datasets, using tools such as SQL and Excel to clean and transform data, and using statistical and visualization techniques to uncover patterns and trends (Dong & Triche, 2020). They may also be involved in developing data-driven products or solutions, and may work closely with other stakeholders, such as data scientists and business analysts, to inform decision-making and strategy. The demand for data analysts is high as organizations increasingly recognize the value of data-driven insights and decision-making. Data analysts may work in a variety of settings, such as consulting firms, government agencies, or private organizations, and may have the opportunity to work on a wide range of projects and challenges.
- **Data managers** are responsible for overseeing the collection, storage, and use of data within an organization. They may work in industries such as healthcare, government, or finance, and are responsible for ensuring that data is properly collected, stored, and used within the organization. Data managers may be involved in a range of activities, such as developing data management policies and procedures, implementing data storage and security measures, and working with stakeholders to ensure that data is used ethically and in compliance with relevant laws and regulations (Chang et al., 2019). They may also be involved in the development of data-driven products or solutions, and may work closely with other stakeholders, such as data analysts and data scientists, to support data-driven decision-making and strategy.
- **Research analysts** use research methods and data analysis to gather and interpret information on a particular topic or industry. They may work in industries such as market research, consulting, or government, and are responsible for conducting research and producing insights and recommendations based on their findings (ZipRecruiter, 2022). Research analysts may use a variety of techniques, such as surveys, interviews, and data analysis, to collect and interpret information. They may also be involved in the development of research plans, and may work closely with other stakeholders, such as clients or policy-makers, to communicate their findings and recommendations. Research analysts may work in a variety of settings, such as consulting firms, research organizations, or government agencies, and may have the opportunity to work on a wide range of projects and topics. The role of a research analyst is important in helping organizations and decision-makers make informed decisions based on data and research.

ECONOMIC FUTURES OF DATA

In the future, organizations that are able to effectively leverage data will be well-positioned for success. Data has become a valuable asset for businesses, as it can provide insights into patron behavior, market trends, and operational efficiencies (Kanarkard et al., 2017). By capitalizing on this data, organizations can make informed decisions that drive growth and profitability.

However, realizing the full potential of data requires more than just collecting it. It is also important to ensure the quality of the data and have the necessary skills and resources to effectively analyze and interpret it. Poor quality data can lead to flawed conclusions and decisions, which can have economic consequences. This is particularly important in fields such as finance and healthcare, where accurate data is critical.

To prepare for the economic futures of data, organizations must invest in processes and systems to manage and maintain data quality, as well as develop the necessary skills and expertise to effectively use data to inform decision-making. Those that are able to do so will be well-positioned to capitalize on the opportunities presented by data and thrive in an increasingly data-driven economy.

Additionally, library and information science students should consider pursuing classes in data science as it can enhance their skills and broaden their career opportunities. In today's data-driven economy, knowledge of data science is becoming increasingly valuable, and library and information professionals who have data science skills can be more competitive in the job market. By investing in data science education, library and information science students can prepare for the future of the information profession and be more resilient to technological and economic change.

REFERENCES

Acquisti, A., Taylor, C., & Wagman, L. (2016). The economics of privacy. *Journal of Economic Literature, 54*(2), 442–92.

Al-Khouri, A. M. (2012). Data ownership: Who owns "my data." *International Journal of Management & Information Technology, 2*(1), 1–8.

Amado, A., Cortez, P., Rita, P., & Moro, S. (2018). Research trends on big data in marketing: A text mining and topic modeling based literature analysis. *European Research on Management and Business Economics, 24*(1), 1–7.

Chang, H. C., Wang, C. Y., & Hawamdeh, S. (2019). Emerging trends in data analytics and knowledge management job market: Extending KSA framework. *Journal of Knowledge Management, 23*(4), 664–86.

Chen, H. (2022). *Quality evaluation and improvement* (doctoral dissertation). University of North Texas.

Davenport, T. H., & Patil, D. J. (2012). Data scientist. *Harvard Business Review, 90*(5), 70-76.

Dong, T., & Triche, J. (2020). A longitudinal analysis of job skills for entry-level data analysts. *Journal of Information Systems Education, 31*(4), 312-26.

Fadler, M., & Legner, C. (2022). Data ownership revisited: Clarifying data accountabilities in times of big data and analytics. *Journal of Business Analytics, 5*(1), 123-39.

Federer, L. (2018). Defining data librarianship: A survey of competencies, skills, and training. *Journal of the Medical Library Association, 106*(3), 294-303.

Glassdoor. (2022). *Data librarians*. Retrieved from https://www.glassdoor.com/Job/data-librarian-jobs-SRCH_KO0,14.htm.

Hoofnagle, C. J., van der Sloot, B., & Borgesius, F. Z. (2019). The European Union general data protection regulation: What it is and what it means. *Information & Communications Technology Law, 28*(1), 65-98.

Hummel, P., Braun, M., & Dabrock, P. (2021). Own data? Ethical reflections on data ownership. *Philosophy & Technology, 34*(3), 545-72.

Kanarkard, W., Seemajaruek, C., Pongsuwan, T., & Inlam, T. (2017). Predictive analytic of library patron behavior. In Proceedings of the 3rd International Conference on Communication in Information Processing (pp. 1-5). ACM. https://doi.org/10.1145/3162957.3162961.

Kerber, W. (2016). Digital markets, data, and privacy: Competition law, consumer law and data protection. *Journal of Intellectual Property Law & Practice, 11*(11), 856-66.

Khade, A. A. (2016). Performing customer behavior analysis using big data analytics. *Procedia Computer Science, 79*, 986-92.

Khan, H. R., & Du, Y. (2018). What is a data librarian? A content analysis of job advertisements for data librarians in the United States academic libraries. *IFLA World Library Conference 2018*. Retrieved from https://library.ifla.org/id/eprint/2255.

Koltay, T. (2017). Data literacy for researchers and data librarians. *Journal of Librarianship and Information Science, 49*(1), 3-14.

Lamoreaux, N. R. (2019). The problem of bigness: From Standard Oil to Google. *Journal of Economic Perspectives, 33*(3), 94-117.

Lee, Y. W., Pipino, L. L., Funk, J. D., & Wang, R. Y. (2006). *Journey to data quality*. The MIT Press.

Lerner, A. P. (1934). The concept of monopoly and the measurement of monopoly power. *The Review of Economic Studies, 1*(3), 157-75.

Loertscher, S., & Marx, L. M. (2020). Digital monopolies: Privacy protection or price regulation? *International Journal of Industrial Organization, 71*, article 102623.

Ma, J. (2022). *Regulating data monopolies: A law and economics perspectives*. Springer.

Meyer, M. A. (2019). Healthcare data scientist qualifications, skills, and job focus: A content analysis of job postings. *Journal of the American Medical Informatics Association, 26*(5), 383–91.

Morville, P. (2021). Big architect, little architect. In *Advances in Information Architecture* (pp. 19–21). Springer.

Nolin, J. M. (2020). Data as oil, infrastructure or asset? Three metaphors of data as economic value. *Journal of Information, Communication and Ethics in Society, 18*(1), 28–43.

Orfanidis, L., Bamidis, P. D., & Eaglestone, B. (2004). Data quality issues in electronic health records: An adaptation framework for the Greek health system. *Health Informatics Journal, 10*(1), 23–36.

Semeler, A. R., Pinto, A. L., & Rozados, H. B. F. (2019). Data science in data librarianship: Core competencies of a data librarian. *Journal of Librarianship and Information Science, 51*(3), 771–80.

Small, H., Kasianovitz, K., Blanford, R., & Celaya, I. (2012). What your tweets tell us about you: Identity, ownership and privacy of Twitter data. *International Journal of Digital Curation, 7*(1), 174–97.

Stead, W. W., & Lorenzi, N. M. (1999). Health informatics: Linking investment to value. *Journal of the American Medical Informatics Association, 6*(5), 341–48.

Stucke, M. E., & Grunes, A. P. (2016). *Big data and competition policy*. Oxford University Press.

Tee, S. W., Bowen, P. L., Doyle, P., & Rohde, F. H. (2007). Factors influencing organizations to improve data quality in their information systems. *Accounting & Finance, 47*(2), 335–55.

ZipRecruiter. (2022). *What is a research analyst and how to become one*. Retrieved from https://www.ziprecruiter.com/Career/Research-Analyst/What-Is-How-to-Become.

15

Further Resources for Advancing Your Python Mastery

Python is a powerful and versatile programming language that has many applications in the field of library and information science. It is particularly useful for tasks such as data extraction, manipulation, and analysis, as well as for building custom tools and applications. With Python, library and information professionals can automate routine tasks, extract data from various sources, and analyze data to gain insights and support decision-making. Additionally, Python's flexibility and wide range of libraries and frameworks make it an ideal choice for developing custom tools and applications to support specific needs and workflows. By learning Python, library and information professionals can enhance their skills and capabilities, and better leverage the power of data and technology to support their work.

This book has explored a range of topics related to Python for library and information professionals, including data manipulation and analysis, web scraping, text analysis, and visualization. It has also discussed the ethical considerations that are important when using Python, such as data security, consent, and transparency. From this content, we understand Python to be not only a programming language but a vital toolkit for the future of librarianship and the information professions.

While we believe this book has prepared you well for employing data science principles in your career, many will want to explore further, to continue to push their skills and develop a real expertise in this field. There are many resources we recommend for people who want to learn more about the Python programming language, including:

1. Online tutorials and courses: There are many online tutorials and courses available that can help people learn Python, ranging from beginner-level

introductions to more advanced topics. Some popular resources for online tutorials and courses include Codecademy, Coursera, and edX.
2. Books: There are also many books available on Python, covering a range of topics and skill levels. Some popular books for learning Python include *Learning Python* by Mark Lutz, *Python Crash Course* by Eric Matthes, and *Python for Data Science Handbook* by Jake VanderPlas.
3. Python documentation: The Python documentation is an official resource that provides comprehensive information on the Python programming language and its standard library. It is a good resource for learning about the various features and capabilities of Python.
4. Online communities: There are many online communities and forums where people can ask questions and get help with Python, such as Stack Overflow and Reddit's /r/learnprogramming subreddit. These communities can be a great resource for getting answers to specific questions or for finding additional learning resources.

FUTURE TRENDS IN PYTHON

As the field of library and information science continues to evolve, so does the Python programming language and its ecosystem. Keeping up with the latest trends and developments in Python is essential for staying ahead of the curve and leveraging new tools and technologies in your work. In this section, we will explore some of the future trends in Python and provide strategies for staying informed about these trends.

1. Python Enhancement Proposals (PEPs): PEPs are documents that propose new features, improvements, or changes to the Python language itself (Nand Sharma et al., 2022). By following PEPs, you can gain insights into the direction Python is taking and the upcoming changes that might affect your projects. The official Python website maintains a repository of PEPs, and regularly reviewing them can help you stay informed about the future of the language.
2. Python Community and Conferences: Engaging with the Python community and attending conferences can provide valuable opportunities to learn about emerging trends and connect with experts in the field. PyCon, the largest annual conference for the Python community, features presentations, workshops, and panel discussions on various Python-related topics (PyCon, 2023). Similarly, local Python user groups and meet-ups offer opportunities to network and share knowledge with like-minded individuals. Participating in these events can expose you to the latest advancements and practices in Python.

3. Online Resources and Newsletters: Numerous online resources and newsletters focus specifically on Python and provide regular updates on the latest trends, libraries, frameworks, and tools. Websites like Python.org, Real Python, Towards Data Science, and Python Weekly offer tutorials, articles, and news on Python-related topics. Subscribing to newsletters such as *Python Weekly* and *Python Bytes* can deliver curated content and updates directly to your inbox, ensuring you stay informed about the evolving Python landscape.
4. Social Media and Online Forums: Social media platforms like Twitter, LinkedIn, and Reddit can serve as valuable sources of information and discussion on Python. Following influential Python developers, open-source projects, and organizations can provide insights into the latest developments and trends. Participating in Python-related discussions on forums like Reddit's /r/Python or Stack Overflow can help you stay informed and get answers to your questions.
5. Blogs and Technical Publications: Many experts and enthusiasts in the Python community maintain blogs and write technical articles on Python-related topics. By following prominent blogs and publications like Python Software Foundation's blog, medium publications like Towards Data Science and Analytics Vidhya, or personal blogs of Python experts, you can access in-depth articles, tutorials, and analyses of emerging trends, libraries, and techniques.
6. Continuous Learning and Online Courses: Invest in continuous learning by enrolling in online courses or programs that focus on Python and data science. Platforms like Coursera, edX, and DataCamp offer courses on Python programming, data analysis, machine learning, and other advanced topics. These courses often cover the latest trends and technologies, providing you with up-to-date knowledge and skills.
7. Open-Source Contributions and Projects: Contributing to open-source projects or starting your own can deepen your understanding of Python and its evolving ecosystem. By actively participating in open-source communities like GitHub, you can collaborate with developers from around the world and gain exposure to cutting-edge projects. Monitoring and contributing to popular libraries or frameworks can provide firsthand experience with emerging trends and practices (Cabo, 2018).

By regularly exploring these resources and engaging with the Python community, you can stay informed about the latest trends, libraries, frameworks, and tools in Python. Remember to allocate time for continuous learning, attend relevant conferences and meet-ups, and actively participate in discussions. Embracing these strategies will help you navigate the evolving Python landscape and maintain your expertise as a library and information professional.

PRACTICE/SAMPLE DATASETS

In addition to learning Python programming concepts and techniques, it is crucial to apply your knowledge to real-world datasets to solidify your skills and gain practical experience. By working with practice/sample datasets, you can enhance your proficiency as a Python programmer and develop a deeper understanding of data manipulation, analysis, and visualization. This section presents a partial listing of datasets that are readily available for you to explore. Please note that some of these resources may require you to create a free account to access the datasets.

INSTITUTE OF MUSEUM AND LIBRARY SERVICES

- Public Library Survey: This dataset, available in CSV or SPSS format, offers information on public libraries across the United States. It covers aspects such as library demographics, services, collections, and more. You can access the dataset through the following link: Public Library Survey.
- State Library Administrative Agency Survey: This dataset, also available in CSV or SPSS format, focuses on state library administrative agencies. It provides data on the services, budgets, staffing, and resources of these agencies. You can find the dataset at: State Library Administrative Agency Survey.
- Museum Data: This dataset, available in CSV format, offers insights into the operations and collections of museums. It covers various aspects such as museum types, attendance, revenue, and more. To explore this dataset, visit: Museum Data.
- Heritage Health Information Survey: Focusing on heritage health information, this dataset (in CSV format) provides information on how libraries support health-related services and resources. It offers valuable data for exploring the intersection of libraries and healthcare. You can access the dataset through: Heritage Health Information Survey.
- Social Wellbeing (Role of Libraries in Their Communities): This dataset, in CSV format, investigates the role of libraries in promoting social wellbeing in their communities. It offers insights into the social impact of libraries and their engagement with community development. Access the dataset here: Social Wellbeing Dataset.
- State Economic and Broadband Availability and Adoption: This dataset, available in XLS format, explores the economic status and broadband availability and adoption at the state level. It can provide valuable context when examining libraries' roles within their broader economic and technological environments. The dataset can be found at: State Economic and Broadband Availability and Adoption.

NATIONAL CENTER FOR EDUCATION STATISTICS

- IPEDS (Integrated Postsecondary Education Data System): IPEDS provides a comprehensive dataset that allows you to compare institutions based on different variables related to academic libraries. By accessing the "Compare Institutions" page on the IPEDS Data Center website, you can explore data on multiple factors, including:
    - Is the library collection entirely electronic?
    - Number of branches of the library
    - Does the library support virtual reference services?
    - Collections: Number of physical and digital resources
    - Expenditures: Total, materials purchasing, salaries and benefits for employees
    - Circulations: Physical, digital, total, interlibrary loan
    - Staffing: Number of full-time equivalent (FTE) staff, number of student assistants
- The dataset is available in CSV format, enabling you to easily import and analyze the data using Python. Moreover, the IPEDS dataset facilitates convenient comparisons between institutions, allowing you to assess library performance in relation to other institutional-level data available within the same system. To access the IPEDS Data Center and explore the dataset, visit: IPEDS Data Center.

AMERICAN LIBRARY ASSOCIATION'S ACCREDITED PROGRAM DATA

The American Library Association (ALA) provides data on accredited library programs, offering insights into faculty, student enrollment, expenditures, and income. Although the dataset is only available in XLS format, it can still be utilized for analysis in conjunction with Python. The data includes the following information:

- Full-time equivalent (FTE) faculty
- Total student enrollment for the department
- Total student enrollment for only the ALA accredited master's programs
- Minority enrollment
- Total expenditures
- Total income

Access the dataset and explore the trended data option through the ALA's Accredited Program Data page: ALA Accredited Program Data.

ALISE DATASET ON LIS SCHOOLS

The Association for Library and Information Science Education (ALISE) provides a statistical report dataset focused on LIS (library and information science) schools. Please note that this dataset is available only for full ALISE members, excluding student members. While the specifics of the dataset may vary, it offers insights into various aspects of LIS schools, such as enrollment, faculty, and more. Explore the dataset through the ALISE Statistical Report page: ALISE Dataset on LIS Schools.

OCLC

OCLC offers datasets that can be valuable for understanding voter perceptions of libraries, providing insights into public opinion and funding. The dataset, available in XLS format, can be accessed through the "From Awareness to Funding—Voter Perceptions of Libraries Data" page on the OCLC website: OCLC Voter Perceptions of Libraries Data.

LIBRARY OF CONGRESS

The Library of Congress offers various dataset repositories that contain a wealth of information related to the storage of resources. These repositories include datasets on historical newspapers, census data, labor data, bibliographic data, and more. You can explore these datasets by visiting the Library of Congress's dataset repositories page: Library of Congress Dataset Repositories.

BIBLIOGRAPHIC DATA

Web of Science: Web of Science provides detailed publication information that is widely used for scientometric studies. While the available dataset formats may vary, you can obtain comprehensive bibliographic data for analysis. Explore the Web of Science dataset through their platform: Web of Science.

Ebsco Databases: Ebsco offers a range of databases with high-quality information, albeit with less extensive coverage compared to broader sources. These databases often focus on specific topics, providing valuable resources for research and analysis. Explore the available Ebsco databases and their content through the Ebsco website: Ebsco Databases.

UNITED STATES CENSUS

The United States Census Bureau provides extensive information about service populations, demographics, and socioeconomic factors. Their datasets can be highly valuable when studying libraries and their communities. Although registration is required, it is free and grants you access to a wealth of data. You can sign up and explore the datasets through the United States Census website: United States Census Data.

ADDITIONAL WEB DATA SOURCES FOR LIBRARIES' DATA

In addition to the aforementioned datasets, there are several other web data sources that provide valuable library-related datasets. These sources offer a wide range of datasets covering various aspects of library resources, usage, and more. Here are a few notable ones:

- Data World for Libraries: Data World is a platform that hosts a vast collection of datasets, including over 145 library datasets. These datasets cover different areas such as library collections, patron usage, circulation data, and more. By exploring Data World for Libraries, you can discover and access a diverse range of datasets that can enhance your understanding of library operations and trends.
- Minitab Dataset Libraries: Minitab Dataset Libraries offer a search and retrieval feature, allowing you to find the right dataset for your specific needs. While not exclusively focused on libraries, Minitab provides datasets that can be relevant for library analysis. By utilizing their search functionality, you can explore and obtain datasets related to libraries, which can then be used for analysis and insights.
- World Library Dataset: The World Library Dataset provides an opportunity to download datasets across different categories related to library resources. These categories may include data on books, publications, libraries' geographic locations, and more. By accessing the World Library Dataset, you can explore and download datasets that align with your specific areas of interest or research.
- Kaggle Library Users Dataset: Kaggle, a popular platform for data science and machine learning, also hosts datasets related to libraries. Their Library Users Dataset section allows you to search for the specific type of library data you are looking for. Whether it's user demographics, circulation data, or other library-related information, Kaggle offers a diverse range of datasets contributed by the data science community.
- National Data About Public Libraries: The National Data About Public Libraries resource provides access to various datasets related to public libraries. On their webpage, you will find multiple links that lead to specific datasets covering different aspects of public library operations, services, and demographics. By clicking on each link, you can access and download the related dataset, enabling you to explore and analyze national-level data about public libraries.

By utilizing these additional web data sources, you can expand your access to diverse library datasets and gain a broader perspective on library-related trends, patterns, and user behavior. These datasets can be valuable assets for Python programmers seeking to enhance their analysis and develop data-driven insights in the library domain.

In conclusion, we hope this book has provided readers with a solid foundation in Python programming and data analysis. We would, of course, love to hear from any readers who found this book helpful in mastering Python concepts and using them in their LIS career! With the skills and knowledge acquired from this book, we believe that readers will be well-equipped to tackle the challenges of working with data in their future careers as information professionals. Whether you are a librarian, archivist, data scientist, or information manager, Python's versatility and widespread use make it a valuable tool to have in your toolkit. We hope the principles and techniques covered in this book will serve as a guide for you as you continue to learn and grow as an information professional.

REFERENCES

Cabo, C. (2018). Effectiveness of flowcharting as a scaffolding tool to learn Python. *IEEE Frontiers in Education Conference.* https://doi.org/10.1109/FIE.2018.8658891.

Nand Sharma, P., Tony Roy Savarimuthu, B., & Stanger, N. (2022). Unearthing open source decision-making processes: A case study of Python enhancement proposals. *Software: Practice and Experience, 52*(10), 2312–46.

PyCon. (2023). What is PyCon US? Retrieved from https://us.pycon.org/2023/about/pycon/.

Glossary

Arguments: Values passed to a function or method that customize its behavior.
Attribute: Represents the state of an object.
Big data: Large and complex datasets that are difficult to process and analyze using traditional data processing methods.
Class: A user-defined data type in object-oriented programming that acts as a template definition of methods and attributes of an individual object.
Code maintenance: The ongoing process of updating, modifying, and fixing existing code.
Consent: The process of obtaining permission from individuals before collecting, using, or sharing their personal data.
Data accuracy: The quality of data being free from errors and representing the true state of affairs.
Data confidentiality: The requirement to keep data secure and confidential, limiting access to authorized individuals.
Data ethics: The principles and practices that govern the responsible and ethical collection, use, and sharing of data.
Data explosion: The rapid and exponential increase in the amount of data being generated, collected, and stored.
Data files: Computer files that contain data in various formats and serve as repositories for storing and retrieving data.
Data librarianship: A role that combines traditional library tasks with data science and management tasks. Data librarians are responsible for managing and organizing data collections, assisting users in finding and using data, and providing data literacy education and training.
Data privacy: The protection of personal and sensitive information from unauthorized access or disclosure.
Data revolution: The rapid growth and transformation of data-driven technologies, practices, and applications that have revolutionized industries and organizations worldwide.
Data science: The field of study that involves extracting insights and knowledge from large datasets using various techniques such as data mining, machine learning, and statistical analysis.
Data security: Measures and practices implemented to protect data from unauthorized access, theft, or misuse.

Data types: The different categories of data that Python supports, such as numeric, sequence, mapping, and set data types.
Debugging: The process of identifying and resolving errors or bugs in code by analyzing and manipulating its execution.
Encapsulation: Bundling data and methods into an object, hiding implementation details and providing a defined interface.
Extreme automation: The use of advanced technologies, such as AI platforms, to automate tasks and decision-making processes.
Function: A named block of code that performs a specific task or set of instructions.
Functional programming: A programming paradigm that emphasizes the use of functions to perform computations, often with an emphasis on immutability.
Inheritance: Mechanism where a subclass inherits properties and behaviors from a superclass.
Library and information science: The field of study and practice concerned with the organization, management, and retrieval of information resources in libraries and other information organizations.
Method: A function that is defined within a class and describes the behavior of an object.
Numeric data types: Includes integers, floats, and complex numbers.
Numpy: A fundamental library for numerical computing in Python, providing data structures like arrays and matrices along with mathematical functions.
Object: An instance of a class that consists of methods and properties created with specifically defined data.
Object-oriented programming: A programming paradigm that involves organizing code into objects that contain both data and methods for utilizing the data.
Polymorphism: The ability of an object to take on multiple forms or have multiple behaviors.
Procedural programming: A programming paradigm that focuses on executing code step-by-step using procedures or functions.
Programming paradigms: Different approaches and styles for organizing and structuring code, such as procedural programming, functional programming, and object-oriented programming.
Python programming language: A high-level, general-purpose programming language known for its versatility and readability. It is widely used in various domains, including web development, data analysis, machine learning, and automation.
Standard Development Kit (SDK): A set of tools and libraries that enable the development and deployment of Python applications.
Testing: The process of evaluating a software system or its components to ensure that they function correctly and meet the specified requirements.
Troubleshooting: The process of identifying and resolving problems or issues in software or hardware systems.
Workspace: The digital environment that allows for the design, development, and execution of Python code.

Index

abstract classes, 21-23
Abstract Syntax Tree, 5
abstraction, 21-22
algorithms, ix, 28, 30, 33-35, 57, 61-64, 104, 112-14, 117
    Brute Force, 33
    Divide and Conquer, 33
    Dynamic, 33
    Graph, 33
    Greedy, 33
    Recursion, 33, 37, 43-44
    Searching, 33, 44
    Sorting, 33-35, 38, 44-45, 63-64
applications, 5, 79, 94, 111, 147
args, 37, 42-43
arguments, 38-39, 41-43
artificial intelligence, 79, 111, 117, 134
attributes (in Python), 3, 13-14, 16, 19-21
automation, vii-viii, 127, 133-34

big data, 121-22, 124-27
binary files, 49
Boolean data, 28-29
boundary conditions, 58
byte code, 5

chatbots, viii, 111
ChatGPT, 111, 133-135
classes (use in Python), 3, 13-14, 16, 18-19, 21-23, 25, 57
code expansion, 14
code maintenance, 14
code organization, 13, 16, 37, 46
code scalability, 13, 34, 58, 63
complex numbers, 27

complex objects, 23
complexity
    time, 30-31, 33-34, 62
    space, 28, 33-34, 62
composition, 23-24
computational efficiency, 30, 33
concrete classes, 21-23
confidentiality, 108, 129-32, 135
copyright, 84, 108, 134
cyberattacks, 131

data analyst, 78, 88, 122, 127, 142
data analytics, 102, 125-27
data breaches, 130-31
data ethics, 129-32, 133, 135
data exchange, 48, 138
data explosion, x, 121-22
data files, ix, 47-54
    appending, 52-53
    deleting, 52
    updating, 52-53
data growth, 123
data literacy, x, 122, 137, 140
data manipulation, viii, 27, 86, 147, 150
data misuse, 131
data ownership, 132, 137-38
data preprocessing, 48, 77, 116
data privacy, 129, 135
data science, vii, 85, 88, 108-9, 127, 137, 140-41, 143, 147-48, 153
data scientist, x, 88, 96, 121, 127, 141-42, 154
data set, 69, 81, 108, 121
data storytelling, 125
data structures, 28, 30-31, 34, 49-50, 57, 61-63, 85, 116

data transformation, 48
data types, ix, 3, 14, 27-30, 35, 48, 59, 141
data visualization, 103, 107, 141
Data.gov, 125-26
debugging, 7, 9-10, 60-61, 64
dictionaries, 27-30, 96

encapsulation, 13, 19-20
errors
   logic, 6, 59-60
   memory, 60
   semantic, 59
   syntax, 59
extensions (for Python programming), 7, 9-10

file formats, viii, 47-50, 54
floats, 27-28
Fourth Industrial Revolution, 127
function calling, 33, 44, 64-65
functions, vii, ix, 3-4, 13-14, 19, 27, 35, 37-46, 48-51, 57, 81, 88
   factorial, 44
   Lambda, 44-46

General Data Protection Regulation (GDPR), 130

Health Insurance Portability and Accountability Act (HIPAA), 130

information architect, 141
information need, 91-92, 112, 134
information professions, 140, 147
inheritance, 13, 16-17, 23
Institute of Museum and Library Services, 69-70, 77, 121, 150
integers, 14, 27-29, 59, 85
integrated development environment, 7, 9
interpreter, 5-7, 9

Jupyter Notebook, 7, 10, 78

Kaggle, 153
kwargs, 37, 42-43

LEGB Rule, 37, 40
librarians, vii-viii, x, 65, 70-73, 76-77, 83, 91-93, 95, 98-99, 101-2, 114-15, 122, 124-25, 129, 134, 154
   data librarians, 88, 121, 137, 140-41
libraries (use in Python), 3, 104-5
library and information science, v, ix-x, 65, 79, 101-5, 107-9, 122, 141, 143, 147-48, 152
Library of Congress, 152

machine learning, vi-vii, 85, 103, 107, 111-13, 117, 124, 126, 134, 141, 149, 153
   reinforcement learning, 113, 117
   supervised, 112
   unsupervised, 112
metadata, viii, 5, 49-50, 82-84, 122, 124-25
monopolies, 137, 139-40

National Center for Education Statistics (NCES), 69
needs analysis, 125
non-primitive data, 27-28
Numpy (Python library), vi-viii, 49, 74, 77, 101-3

Object-Oriented Programming, vii, ix, 3, 13-15, 25, 27
objects (in Python), vii, 3-4, 13-14, 17, 19, 21, 23-25, 78, 86
open-source, vi, 3, 149
optimization, 64, 112
OS module, 53-54

Pandas (Python library), vi-viii, 49-53, 71, 74, 77-78, 84, 87, 101-4
parent classes, 16-19
performance optimization, 64, 112
personal data, 108, 130, 132, 140
plugins (for use in Python), 7, 9
polymorphism, 17-18
primitive data, 27-28
profilers, 57, 64-65
Python programming language, v, ix-x, 3-9, 37, 86, 94, 147-48

ranges, 27
readability, 45
regression, 58-59, 69, 73-76, 88, 112, 114
research analyst, 86-87, 142
reusability, 21, 37, 46, 86

scope, 39-40, 46
search engine, 38
sentiment analysis, viii, 93, 95-99
social media, 95-96, 102, 104, 107, 111, 122-23, 126, 138, 149
source code, vi, 5-6, 78, 84
Standard Development Kit, 7
statistics, 69, 107, 112, 141, 151
subclasses, 16-19, 21-23
syntax (for Functions), vii, 5-6, 16, 18, 37-38, 42, 45-46, 59, 88

testing, 7, 10, 57-60, 63
   Acceptance, 58
   Functional, 58
   Integration, 57-58
   Performance, 58, 63

Regression, 58
Security, 58-59
text Analysis, x, 65, 79, 91-98, 101-2, 104-5
text mining, viii, 94
transparency, 129, 133, 140
troubleshooting, 3, 57, 59
tuples, 27, 29-30
Turing Test, 134

usage data, x, 65
user behavior, viii

VADER, 96, 99
versatility, vi-vii, 125
Visual Studio Code, 10
visualization (Data analysis and), vi-vii, 50, 78, 93, 101-3, 107, 141-42, 147, 150

web scraping, viii, 101-2, 106-7, 147
workflows, viii, 113, 147

XML, 49, 102, 126

About the Authors

Brady D. Lund, PhD, is an assistant professor of information science at the University of North Texas. He has published four books related to technology in libraries and educational institutions—including *Casting Light on the Dark Web* and *Creating Accessible Online Instruction Using Universal Design Principles*, both for Rowman & Littlefield Publishing—and over one hundred articles, editorials, and opinion papers. His work often combines data analytics principles with library and information science research topics.

Daniel Agbaji is a PhD student in information science at the University of North Texas, with a concentration in data science. As an experienced researcher and software developer, he has written scholarly publications and book chapters with notable publishers. Daniel has published articles in the information science and library field. As a software developer, Daniel has written thousands of lines of code for Fortune 500 companies.

Kossi Dodzi Bissadu is a PhD student in information science at the University of North Texas, with a major in cybersecurity. He currently works as a software engineer at Zenner USA, where he leads various products, software, applications, and systems development projects. He is also a U.S. Air Force veteran, a very talented and dedicated professional who has more than ten years of professional record achievements, and he has demonstrated success leading, managing, and working in technology and sciences. He has developed several applications, websites, APIs, and services using various programming languages, including Python. He has also published several research papers and served as a reviewer for two international journals.

Haihua Chen, PhD, is an assistant professor of data science at the University of North Texas, with extensive experience in Python and teaching technical courses for information science and data science students. He has published nearly fifty articles on various topics, including natural language processing, machine learning, data quality, information retrieval, digital libraries, and applied data science. Dr. Chen is the editor of *The Electronic Library*. He has served on organizing committees for international conferences and workshops.

www.ingramcontent.com/pod-product-compliance
Lightning Source LLC
Chambersburg PA
CBHW051614230426
43668CB00013B/2107